Aubrey Beardsley

DECADENCE & DESIRE

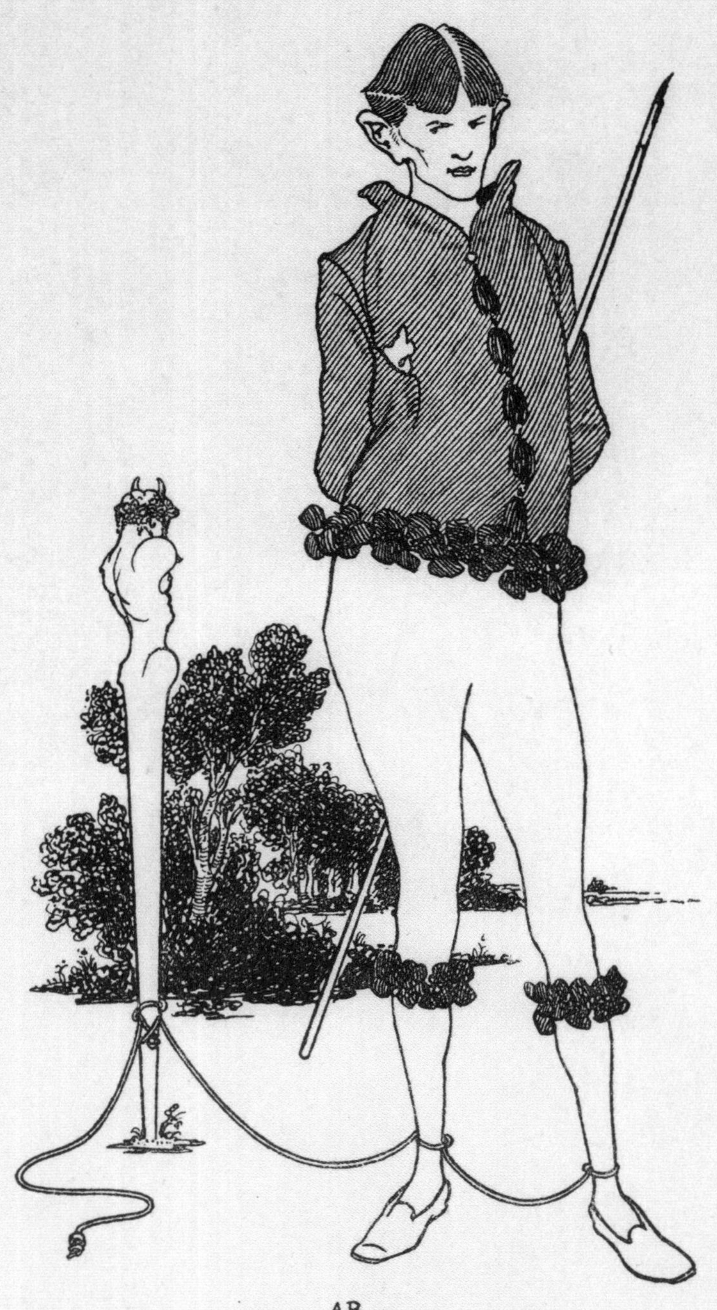
AB

Aubrey Beardsley

DECADENCE & DESIRE

Jan Marsh

Thames & Hudson | V&A

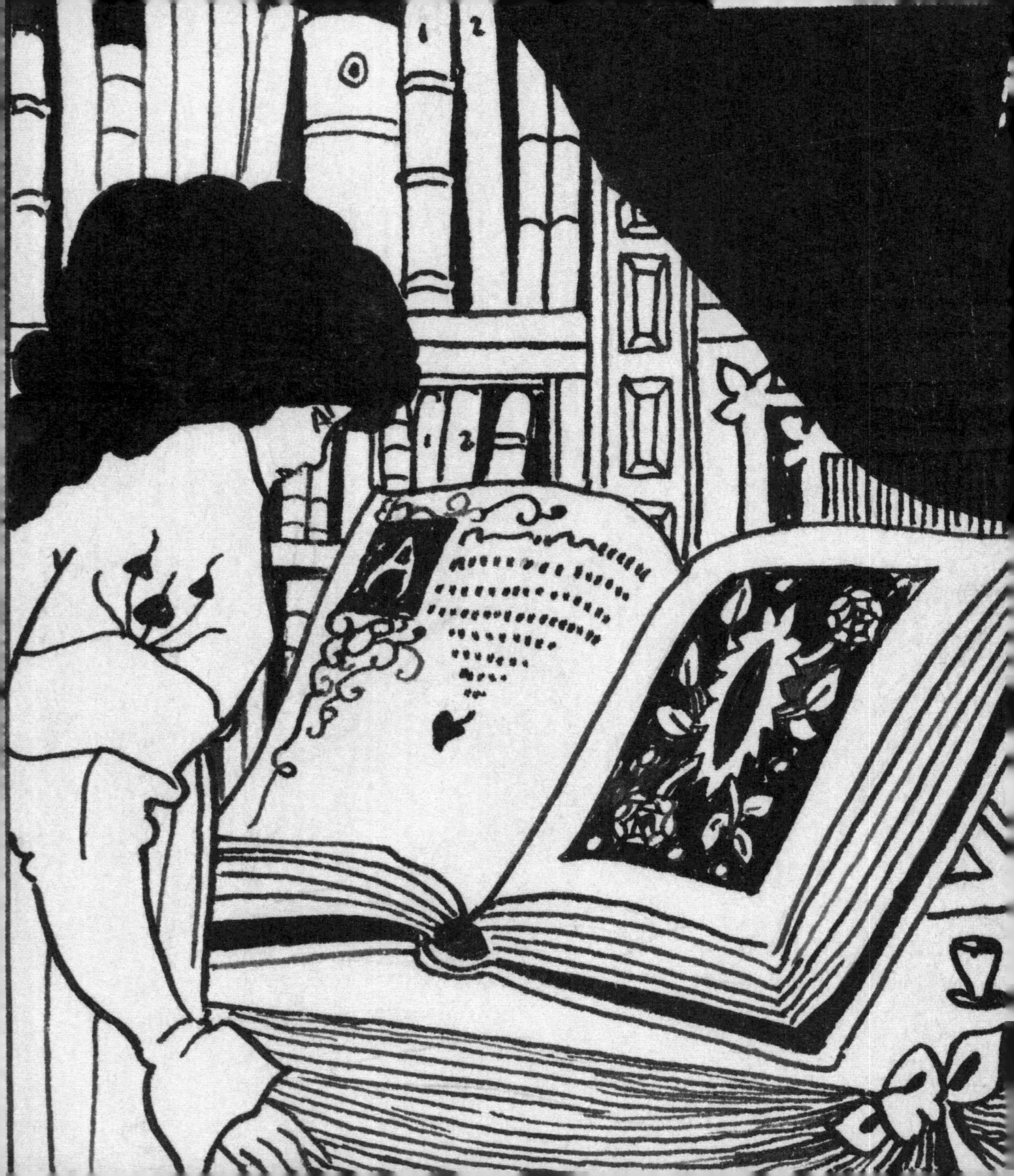

Contents

Preface

Aubrey Beardsley (1872–1898) was an artist whose illustrative work burned sharply, with bright incandescence, but briefly, until his death aged just 25. To many, he and his art personify the *fin de siècle* 1890s, 'the Beardsley age' of Decadence, of the rejection of moral and aesthetic convention in favour of perversity and scepticism, and of delight in the exotic, the scandalous, the sensational. Baudelaire and Verlaine, Edgar Allan Poe and Oscar Wilde were literary models, while Gustave Moreau, Toulouse-Lautrec and Fernand Khnopff were among the artists of the period.

The Gothick element – the spelling indicating modern uses of medieval decorative forms, tending to the grotesque and anarchic – is strong, even dominant, in the work of Beardsley. True, his approach is sophisticated and refined, the lines elegant and the subjects often classical, but Beardsley's treatment of them is subversive, provocative and frequently obscene. These contradictions lie at the heart of Beardsley's aesthetic appeal, as visual pleasure is both undercut and enhanced by ugly content, eliciting a shiver of disgusted delight.

Offset by piquant details, the graphic eloquence of black and white space in Beardsley's art is unmistakeably individual and original. It is also absolutely of its time, when the medium of dramatic monochrome design in lithograph printing flourished in books, posters and advertisements (fig. 1). At the same moment a world-weary mood swept through European culture, blending the pursuit of intense, amoral experience, leisured caprice and the valorization of transgressive social and sexual preferences. Perversity became fashionable.

One of Beardsley's earliest commissions visually catches this trend in a series of 130 small designs, 'fanciful grotesques, little more than doodles',[1] made to decorate humorous collections of eighteenth-century wit entitled *Bon-Mots* [*sic*]. In the tradition of medieval illumination, Hieronymus Bosch's fantastical creatures, Henry Fuseli's nightmares and Edward Lear's comic animals, Beardsley drew satyrs, hermaphrodites, pierrots, chimeras, embryos, monsters, monkeys and spitting cats. Some were simply variations on taking a line for a walk, in ways that foreshadow his more famous compositions.

His illustrations made the periodical *The Yellow Book* notorious and Oscar Wilde's *Salome* exhilarating, while those drawn for Aristophanes' *Lysistrata* are completely shocking even today and have recently been described as 'elegantly filthy'.[2] Despite their compelling qualities, they remain disliked by many readers, so that Beardsley's reputation is still curiously contentious – as he would surely have relished.

Fig. 1 Detail from *The Lady of the Lake*, 1893–4 (p. 58)

Introduction

'I have one aim – the grotesque. If I am not grotesque I am nothing'[3]

In his iconic portrait by bookseller-turned-photographer Frederick Evans, we see Beardsley's beaked profile cupped in long fingers (fig. 2). Evans said to him: 'There's not much to be done with a face like yours. You're only a gargoyle, you know.' Beardsley put his hands up to his face. 'That's it! a gargoyle on Notre Dame,' exclaimed Evans, seeing the resemblance to a carved devil known as *Le Stryge* (fig. 3). Beardsley was delighted: 'I think the photos are splendid; couldn't be better.'[4]

Of Beardsley, his recent biographer Matthew Sturgis has written: 'Not the least of his creations was himself'; he was an enigmatic 'master of pose, a striker of attitudes … Beardsley adopted his masks not to obscure his personality but to express it.'[5] According to a contemporary, the poet Arthur Symons:

> his conversation had a peculiar kind of brilliance, different in order but scarcely inferior in quality to that of any other contemporary master of that art; a salt, whimsical dogmatism, equally full of convinced egoism and of imperturbable keen-sightedness. Generally choosing to be paradoxical, and vehement on behalf of any enthusiasm of the mind, he was the dupe of none of his own statements, or indeed of his own enthusiasms, and, really, very coldly impartial.
>
> I scarcely except even his own judgment of himself, in spite of his petulant, amusing self-assertion, so full of the childishness of genius. He thought, and was right

Fig. 2 *Aubrey Beardsley*, by Frederick Evans, *c.*1894
Platinum print
The Royal Photographic Society Collection at the Victoria and Albert Museum, London, acquired with the generous assistance of the Heritage Lottery Fund and Art Fund (V&A: RPS.3375-2018)

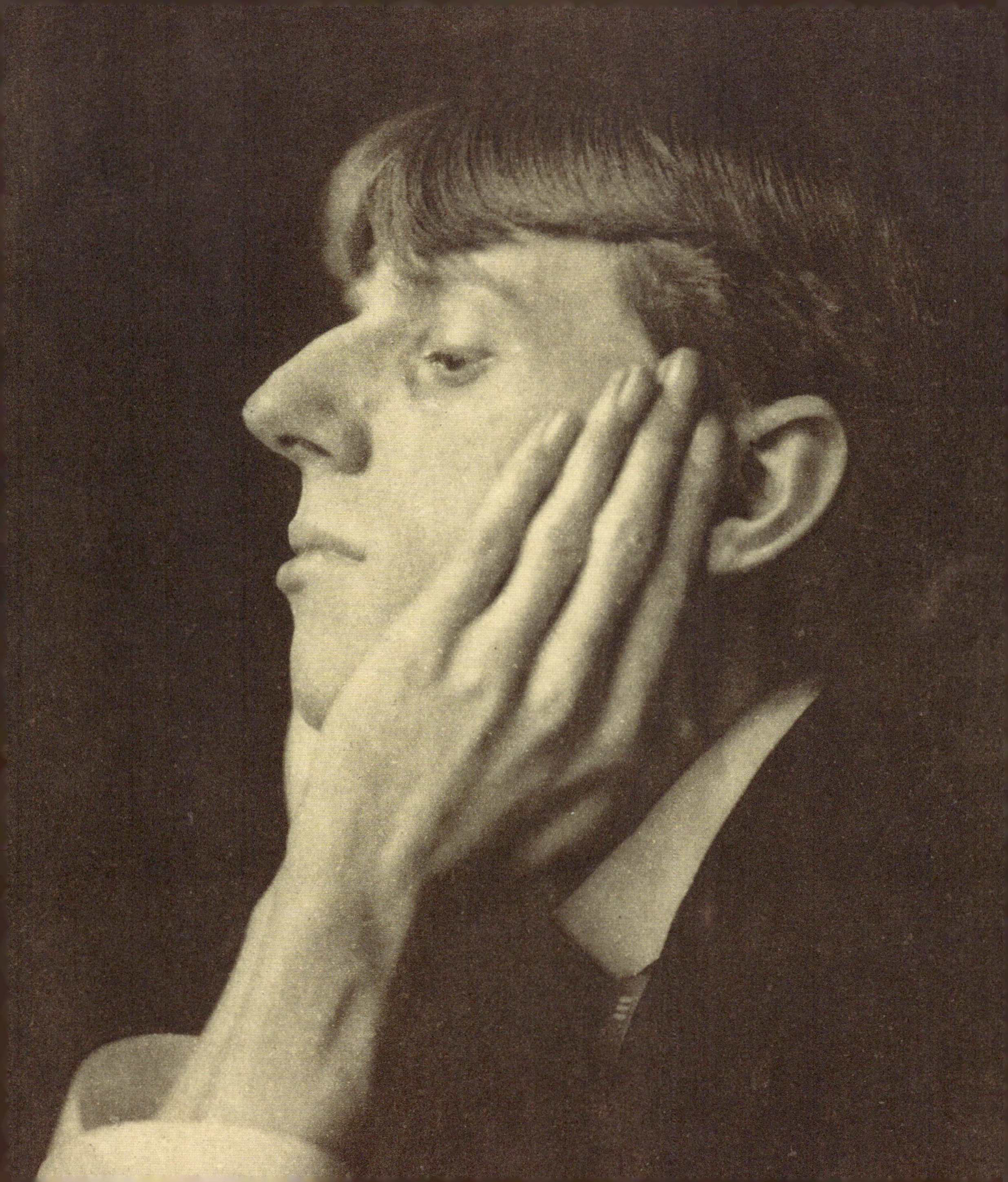

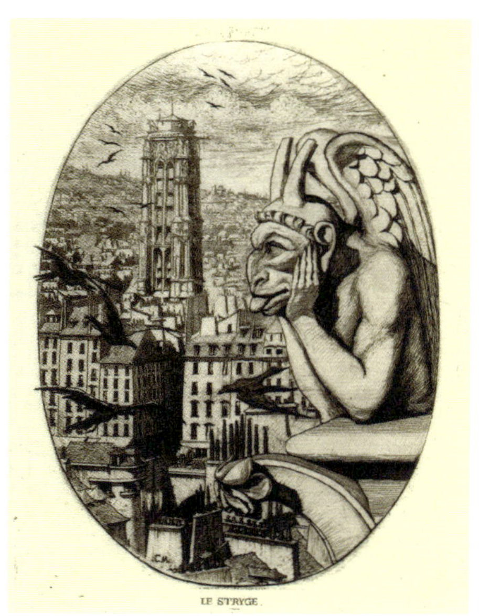

in thinking, very highly of himself; he admired himself enormously; but his intellect would never allow itself to be deceived even about his own accomplishments. This clear, unemotional intellect, emotional only in the perhaps highest sense, where emotion almost ceases to be recognisable, in the abstract, for ideas, for lines, left him, with all his interests in life, with all his sociability, of a sort, essentially very lonely.[6]

Fig. 3 *Le Stryge* (The Vampire), by Auguste Delâtre, 1853
Etching, print on paper
British Museum
(BM: 1880,0612.341)

Fig. 4 *Aubrey Beardsley*, by Jacques-Emile Blanche, 1895
Oil on canvas
National Portrait Gallery, London
(NPG 1991)

Beardsley's self-description was comparably candid. 'I am now eighteen years old,' he wrote in 1891, 'with a vile constitution, a sallow face and sunken eyes, long red hair, a shuffling gait and a stoop.'[7] Oscar Wilde said he had 'a face like a silver hatchet and grass green hair'.[8] However, his portrait by Jacques-Emile Blanche (fig. 4) shows his hair chestnut rather than red, and his

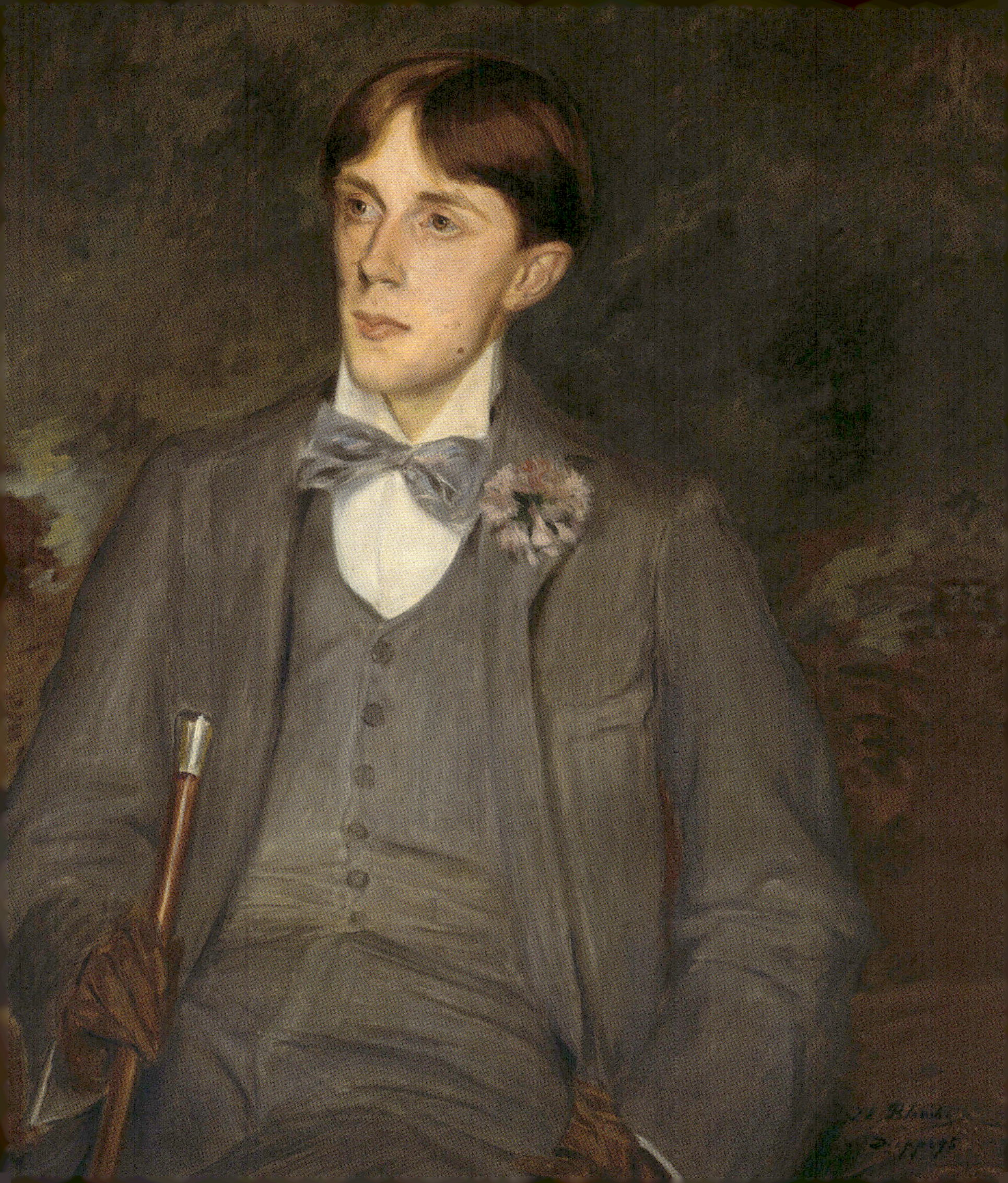

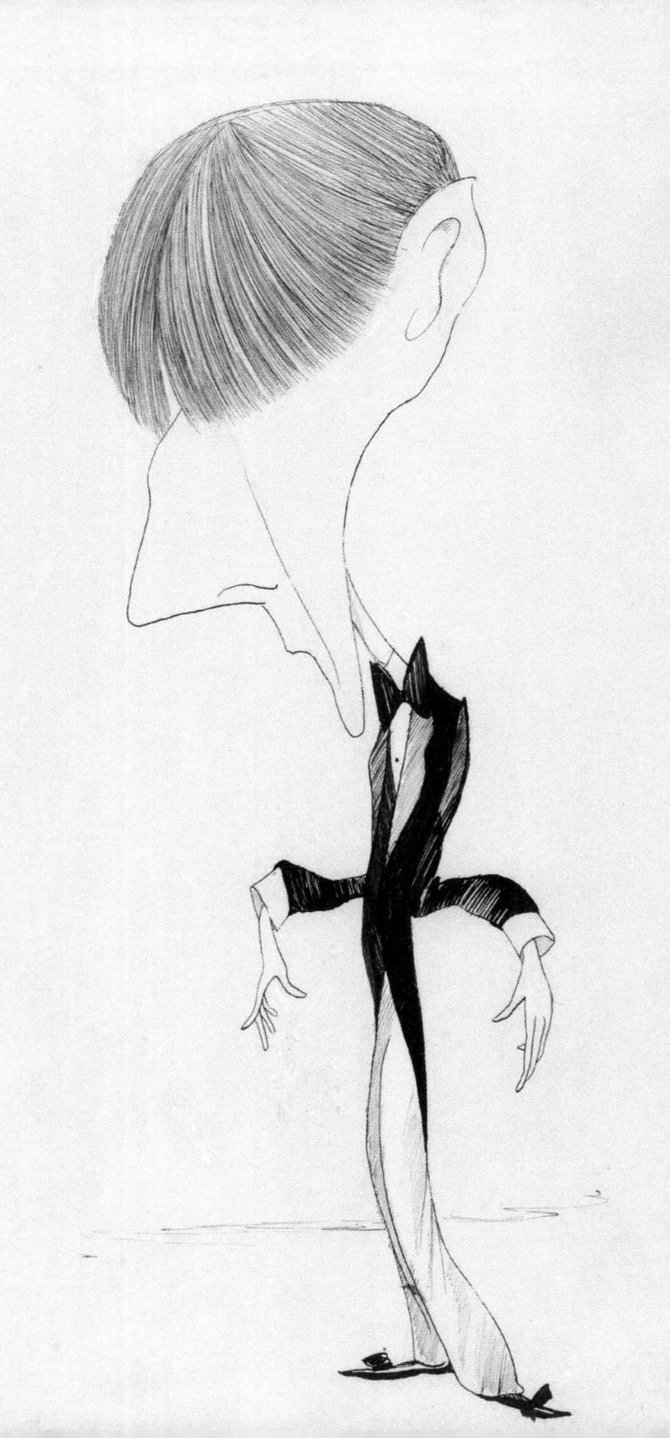

habitually impeccable dress: a grey morning suit for daytime, with buttonhole, cravat, gloves and cane. Together with his tall thin figure and studied courtesy, all created the look of a dandy, as he is personified by Max Beerbohm in a caricature published in 1894 (fig. 5).

Arthur Symons described the paradoxical range of Beardsley's art, where

> the design might be for an edition of a classic or for the cover of a catalogue of second-hand books. And the design might seem to have no relation with the title of its subject, and, indeed, might have none: its relation was of line to line within the limits of its own border, and to nothing else in the world. Thus he could change his whole manner of working five or six times over in the course of as many years, seem to employ himself much of the time on trivial subjects, and yet retain, almost unimpaired, an originality which consisted in the extreme beauty and the absolute certainty of design.[9]

First steps in art

Aubrey Vincent Beardsley was born on 21 August 1872, in Brighton, the second child and only son of parents who held uncertainly to gentility on slender means. His modest inheritance soon spent, his father became a rather incidental figure in the family. Aubrey's mother, the daughter of an Indian Army surgeon, was cultured and ambitious for her children, ensuring their education in music, literature and art, including performance and recitation. Aubrey's sister, Mabel, initially directed into teaching, later turned her ambitions to the stage; she and her brother remained very close.

Aubrey's school fees were paid by a benefactor, but at the age of 16 he took employment as a clerk in London, first with a district surveyor, then with an insurance firm, where his salary helped

Fig. 5 *Aubrey Beardsley*, by Max Beerbohm, *c.*1894
Pen and ink on paper
Victoria and Albert Museum, London (V&A: E.1379-1931)
Given by Mrs G.R. Halkett

maintain the family. His first finished drawings illustrated his reading of French novels and Restoration drama, but the pursuit of work and art was interrupted by haemorrhages, as tubercular infection attacked his lungs.

Thenceforth Beardsley was effectively an invalid. But, as he reported to his former schoolmaster, 'that drawing faculty would come uppermost. So I submit to the inevitable.'[10] Now, influence from the artists Dante Gabriel Rossetti, J.A.M. Whistler and Edward Burne-Jones became visible in his work. The first was a founder member of the Pre-Raphaelite Brotherhood; the latter two were leading figures in the succeeding Aesthetic movement, which from the mid-1870s had been a dominant strand in art, showcased by the fashionable Grosvenor Gallery in London.

In the summer of 1891 Aubrey and Mabel visited the London home of shipowner Frederick Leyland, to see his collection of works by the Pre-Raphaelites. He had also commissioned Whistler to create the famous Peacock Room at the house. On a subsequent weekend the Beardsleys aimed for what they thought was an open afternoon at Burne-Jones's studio. Finding they were mistaken, the young visitors were initially turned away, but then summoned back; as well as welcoming them, Burne-Jones also looked at the portfolio Aubrey always carried with him (fig. 6). Aubrey later described the occasion:

> I can tell you it was an exciting moment when he first opened my portfolio and looked at the first drawings … After he had examined them for a few minutes he exclaimed, 'There is *no* doubt about your gift, one day you will most assuredly paint very great and beautiful pictures.'[11]

Fig. 6 *Perseus with the head of Medusa*, by Aubrey Beardsley, 1891
Line block print
Victoria and Albert Museum, London
(V&A: E.432-1899)

This momentous endorsement launched Beardsley's career. Burne-Jones showed him round the studio, made introductions and recommended formal study at art school. 'Design as much as you

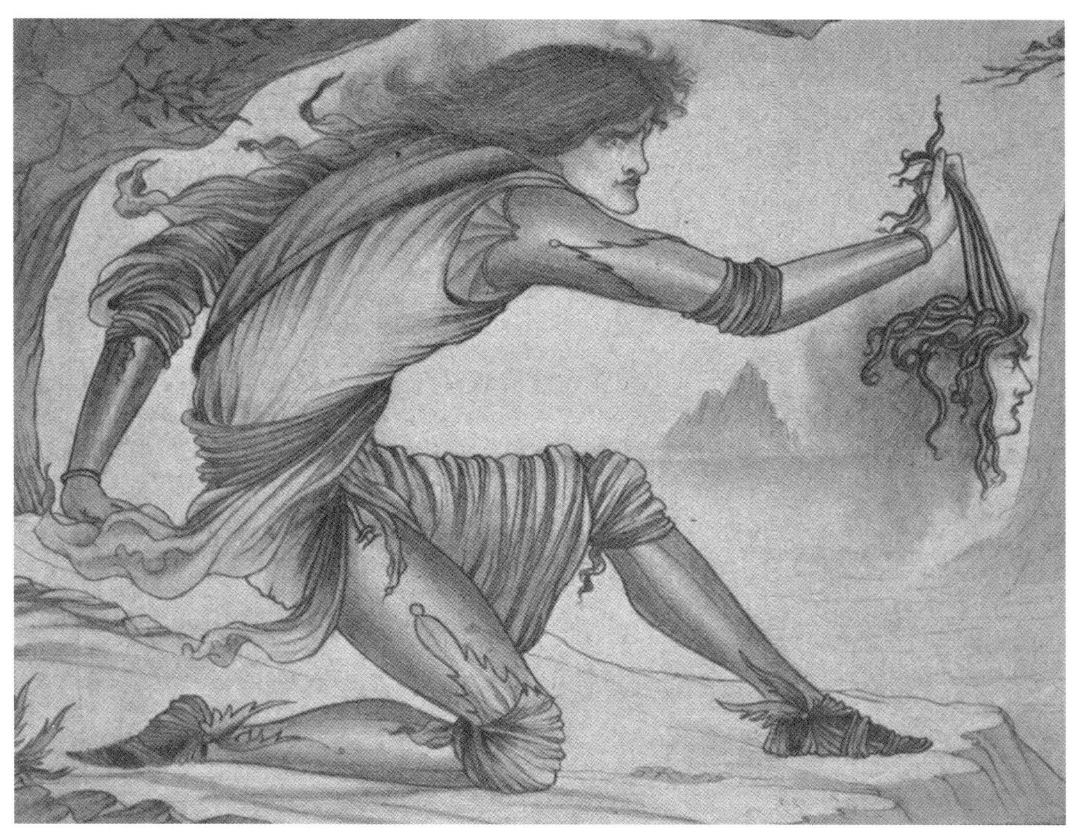

can; your early sketches will be of immense service to you later on. Every one of the drawings you have shown me would make beautiful paintings ... All are *full* of thought, poetry and imagination.'[12]

So Beardsley enrolled for evening sessions at Westminster School of Art under Professor Fred Brown, making careful studies in pencil and charcoal. A contemporary recalled the many plaster casts to be copied there: sculptured angels and chimeras, images of the Crucifixion, a Buddhist or Hindu figure, an Assyrian relief, an actual skeleton with the bones labelled. Brown's teaching emphasized outline, composition and individual expression. Here, Beardsley also discovered the graphic work of the designer and illustrator Walter Crane, and received advice on line drawing in pen and ink. And he was introduced to what would now be called a gay subset of critics and patrons.

Early commissions

If Beardsley had previously aspired to paint 'very great and beautiful pictures', he was diverted back into drawing by a commission from the publishers J.M. Dent to illustrate *Le Morte Darthur*, Sir Thomas Malory's late medieval version of the legends of King Arthur and his knights of the Round Table. Following the style of the books being produced at William Morris's Kelmscott Press, the 'drawings were to be done in medieval manner and there were to be many of them',[13] including elaborate borders, initials and ornaments. The payments for what turned out to be hundreds of decorative items and full-page pictures (**plates 11, 15–22**) enabled Beardsley to quit office work, and would tether him to line drawing for reproduction via process prints and lithography. Known as 'black-and-white' work, this was the medium of the age, as technology developed for illustrated books, magazines and advertisements. Lithography included colour, either in the flat blocks of poster art or the newest forms of four- and five-colour prints, for framing and displaying.

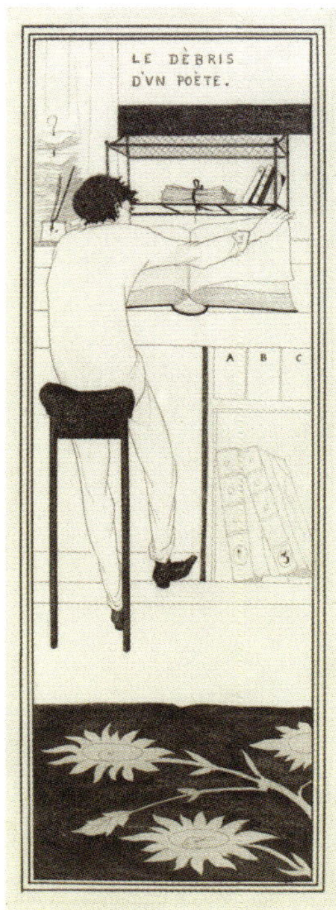

Fig. 7 *Le Dèbris* [sic] *d'un Poète*,
by Aubrey Beardsley, *c*.1892
Pen, Indian ink and wash on paper
Victoria and Albert Museum, London
(V&A: E.1965-1934)
Given by Canon Gray in memory
of André Raffalovich

Beardsley claimed he had besieged and browbeaten publishers with his 'so new and so daringly original' designs (fig. 7), which developed Burne-Jones's linear style with what are called 'hairline' attributes or calligraphic flourishes. These culminated in a large picture of *Siegfried* (10) which was hung in the Burne-Joneses' drawing room.[14] It was also published in *The Studio*, a new journal promoting contemporary art and design. Other commissions followed swiftly, one being for an untitled series of grotesques, another being for the *Vera Historia* by the Greek writer Lucian (23 and 24). These, Beardsley boasted, 'are certainly the most extraordinary things that have ever appeared in a book both in respect of technique and conception. They are also the most indecent. I have thirty little drawings to do for it.'[15] In addition, he had an assignment for a weekly paper, the *Pall Mall Budget* (**6**, **8**), with which he wanted to make 'the old black-and-white duffers sit up', and which featured current theatre productions – the 1890s were also a great decade on the British stage, with actors like Henry Irving and Ellen Terry (fig. 8). 'I have fortune at my foot,' Beardsley crowed, 'Daily I wax greater in facility of execution.'[16]

In June 1893 he and Mabel moved from cramped lodgings to a larger house in Pimlico, then a slightly seedy but artistic quarter, south of Victoria station. The drawing room, where Aubrey worked, had orange walls and black doors, floors and furniture, in homage to the Decadent taste outlined by the French

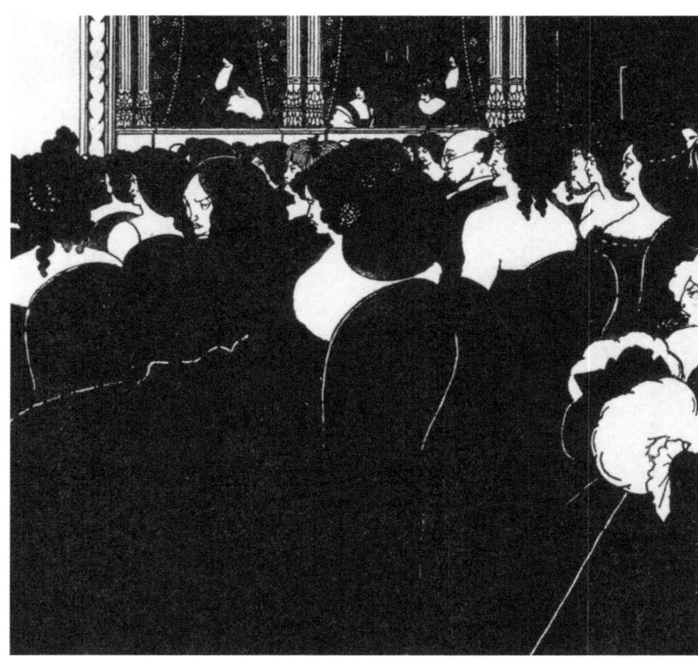

Fig. 8 Detail of *The Wagnerites*, published in *The Yellow Book*, vol. III, 1894
Line block print
Victoria and Albert Museum, London (V&A: E.15-1900)

novelist and art critic Joris-Karl Huysmans, who declared that orange was 'the most morbid and irritating of colours'. Various shades of purple – lavender, mauve, plum – were also Decadent favourites (see for example 38 and 39).

These colours resurfaced in the late 1960s during the art nouveau revival in fashion and graphic art, which also appropriated Beardsley's densely swirling elongations and interlacings in reaction to the typically clean lines of Modernist design. The 1960s revival popularized Beardsley's works as a major element in the counter-culture of the time, with its affirmation of diverse lifestyles, promotion of sexual freedoms and political challenge. A popular exhibition at the Victoria and Albert Museum in 1966 preceded the biographies, catalogues, centenary studies and scholarly research that reconfirmed Beardsley's reputation as a visual artist of notable skill and imagination.

The *Morte Darthur* and other commissions provided invaluable training in design to order, which demanded continuous invention and swift execution. However, although Beardsley insisted that he still clung 'to the best principles of the P.R.B [Pre-Raphaelite Brotherhood]', he was dismayed when William Morris damned his Arthurian imitations. 'The truth is that while *his* work is a mere imitation of the old stuff, mine is fresh and original,' Beardsley riposted combatively.[17] He grew arrogant and ungracious. After Beardsley's death, Burne-Jones recalled a last visit:

> I asked him how he was getting on with the book he was decorating – King Arthur that was – and he said he'd be precious glad when it was done, he hated it so. So I asked him, why did he do it, and he said because he'd been asked. … and I said how could it be successful work then. I never saw such a pitiful exhibition of vanity in my life. I wondered why it was he took the trouble to come and see me, unless it was to shew off and let me know my influence with him was over.[18]

One reason was that, with different possibilities opening for him, Beardsley's visual imagination was racing in various directions, as it would continue to do, stimulated by new subjects and exposure to a wider world of art.

Salome

Through Fred Brown, Beardsley exhibited line drawings at the New English Art Club, an alternative, more 'modern' London venue launched in 1885. One was his first depiction of Salome caressing the head of John the Baptist, which together with other drawings reproduced in *The Studio* led to a commission from the publisher John Lane to illustrate an edition of Oscar Wilde's play *Salome* (1894). First published in French, this dramatizes the biblical legend of the daughter of Herodias who danced before King Herod and gave her mother the opportunity to demand the death of the imprisoned John the Baptist. Beardsley knew Wilde through his new friends Robert Ross, a journalist and art critic, artist Will Rothenstein and caricaturist-cum-dandy Max Beerbohm, and Wilde inscribed a copy of *Salome*, 'for Aubrey: for the only artist who, besides myself, knows what the dance of the seven veils is, and can see that invisible dance'.[19] Wilde also suggested that Salome's face should be different in each picture.

The illustrations (28–37) were in a truly new mode. The swooping lines and variegated patterning reflect Beardsley's latest admiration for Whistler's peacocks and Japanese *shunga* (erotic art) woodblocks respectively, while the compositions, with figures often floating high on the page and clad in garments denoting current fashions, have visual qualities shared with the abrupt shifts and extravagant imagery of Wilde's proto-modern dialogue. Combining the stylish and hieratic with the subversive and distorted, they create dynamic forms of outline offset with briefer passages of solid black. In Beardsley's design for the List of Illustrations (fig. 9), the page format including a panel of text allowed for the asymmetrical composition that became a Beardsley hallmark. Here the sinuous figure of Salome surfaces as if from a pond of stylized flowerets, accompanied by a small bat. Below is a grotesque – part winged and masked Eros, part kneeling goat – reminiscent of the marginal figures in medieval manuscripts.

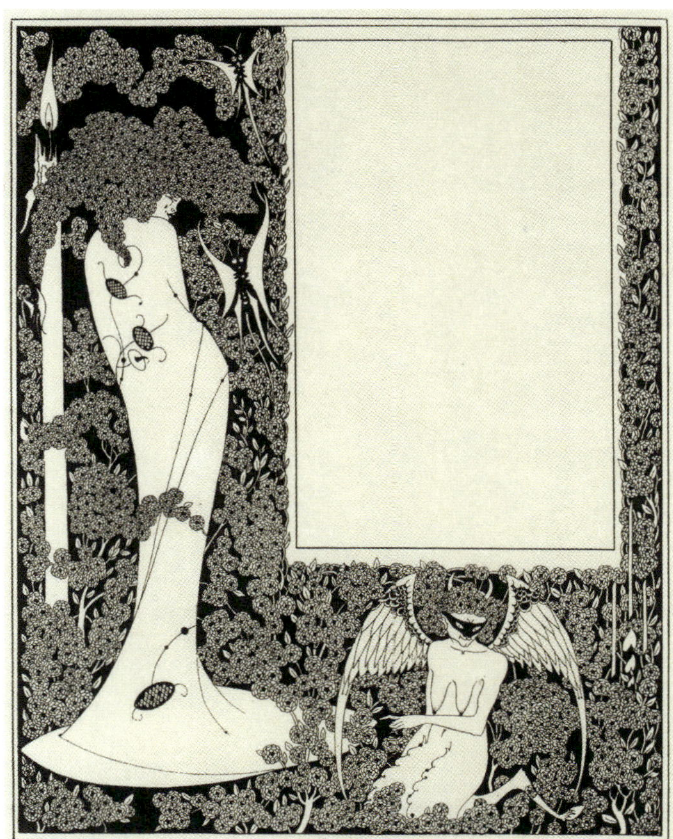

Fig. 9 Design for List of Illustrations, plate IV from *A Portfolio of Aubrey Beardsley's drawings illustrating Salome by Oscar Wilde*, published by John Lane, London, 1907
(first published in 1894)
Line block print on Japanese vellum
Victoria and Albert Museum, London
(V&A: E.425-1972)

SOLD HERE

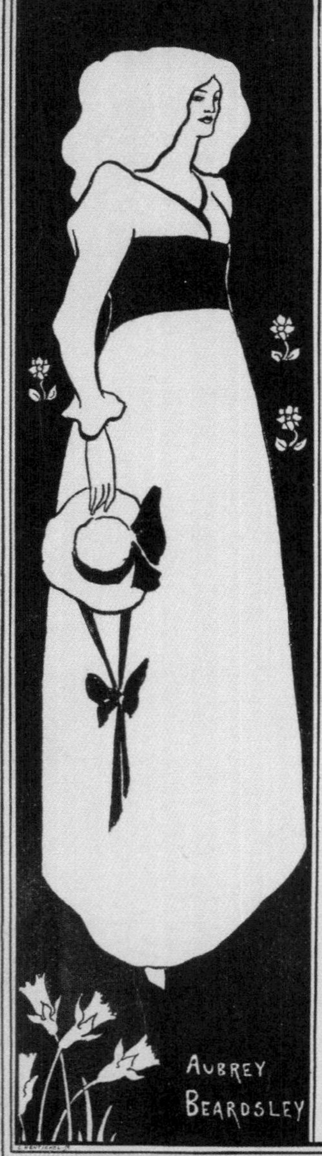

The Yellow Book

Contents of Vol. I

April 1894

Letterpress

I.	The Death of the Lion	By Henry James
II.	Tree-Worship	Richard Le Gallienne
III.	A Defence of Cosmetics	Max Beerbohm
IV.	Δαιμονιζόμενος	Arthur Christopher Benson
V.	Irremediable	Ella D'Arcy
VI.	The Frontier	William Watson
VII.	Night on Curbar Edge	
VIII.	A Sentimental Cellar	George Saintsbury
IX.	Stella Maris	Arthur Symons
X.	Mercedes	Henry Harland
XI.	A Broken Looking-Glass	
XII.	Alere Flammam	Edmund Gosse
XIII.	A Dream of November	
XIV.	The Dedication	Fred M. Simpson
XV.	A Lost Masterpiece	George Egerton
XVI.	Reticence in Literature	Arthur Waugh
XVII.	Modern Melodrama	Hubert Crackanthorpe
XVIII.	London	John Davidson
XIX.	Down-a-down	
XX.	The Love-Story of Luigi Tansillo	Richard Garnett, LL.D.
XXI.	The Fool's Hour	John Oliver Hobbes and George Moore

Pictures

I.	A Study	By Sir Frederic Leighton, P.R.A.
II.	L'Education Sentimentale	Aubrey Beardsley
III.	Le Puy en Velay	Joseph Pennell
IV.	The Old Oxford Music-Hall	Walter Sickert
V.	Portrait of a Gentleman	Will Rothenstein
VI.	The Reflected Faun	Laurence Housman
VII.	Night Piece	Aubrey Beardsley
VIII.	A Study	Sir Frederic Leighton, P.R.A.
IX.	Portrait of a Lady	Will Rothenstein
X.	Portrait of Mrs. Patrick Campbell	Aubrey Beardsley
XI.	The Head of Minos	J. T. Nettleship
XII.	Portrait of a Lady	Charles W. Furse
XIII.	A Lady Reading	Walter Sickert
XIV.	A Book Plate	Aubrey Beardsley
XV.	A Book Plate	R. Anning Bell

London: Elkin Mathews & John Lane

Vigo Street, W

And at all Booksellers and Railway Bookstalls

PRICE FIVE SHILLINGS NET

The sexual element of the Salome illustrations is clearly but coldly conveyed, with naked nipples and naked boys, while the many details (drawn from the text) create tense, unbalanced compositions. Depictions of Wilde as a jester and ringmaster holding his own book (32) and as the Woman in the Moon (28) were surely maliciously intended: Beardsley did not wish to be viewed as the dramatist's acolyte.

Like much of the public and press, *The Times* condemned the illustrations as 'fantastic, grotesque, unintelligible, repulsive. They seem to represent the manners of Judea as conceived by Mr Oscar Wilde, portrayed in the style of the Japanese grotesque as conceived by a French *décadent*. The whole thing must be a joke.'[20] This reception was of course success by scandal. Fame was confirmed by a satirical allusion in *Punch* to a *fin de siècle* illustrator named Mortarthurio Whiskersley. Other parodic names emerged: Weirdly Beardsley, Daubry Beardless.

The Yellow Book

Beardsley's flame continued to blaze with the launch of *The Yellow Book* in spring 1894. Intended as a new form of magazine using the latest image-reproduction technology, its aim was:

> to depart as far as may be from the bad old traditions of periodical literature, and to provide an Illustrated Magazine which shall be beautiful as a piece of book-making, modern and distinguished in its letterpress and its pictures, and withal popular in the better sense of the word. It is felt that such a Magazine, at present, is conspicuous by its absence.
>
> In point of mechanical excellence THE YELLOW BOOK will be as nearly perfect as can be made. ... It will contain 256 pages, or over, and will be bound in limp yellow cloth ... The pictures will in no case serve

Fig. 10 Promotional card for *The Yellow Book*, published by Elkin Matthews and John Lane, London, 1894
Line block and letterpress
Victoria and Albert Museum, London (V&A: 1377-1931)
Given by Mrs G.R. Halkett

> as illustrations to the letter-press, but each will stand by itself as an independent contribution. … In the matter of reproduction care will be taken to secure the finest possible results – results which, it is hoped, will surpass even the best obtained in France and America.'[21]

Beardsley was art editor and principal illustrator. 'Not just a *paper* thing,' he insisted, 'A *bound* thing: a real *book*, bound in good thick boards. *Yellow* ones. Bright yellow.'[22] He was swift to exploit the latest line-block printing process: it enabled him to make dramatic use of black and white space, as deployed for example in a promotional card for the publication (fig. 10) to add a sinister note to a pastoral image, while the 'portrait' page format of most books and journals lent itself well to elongated vertical compositions, which contributed to the emerging art nouveau graphic style. Generally, Beardsley's designs (40–44) purposefully represented 'modern life, modern dress, modern costume' and modern celebrities like actor Mrs Patrick Campbell, together with images of London's nightlife that suggested the strolling harlotry of theatreland. Large areas of black played off against fine white lines to suggest locations of 'half-hidden but always present urban depravity', giving the designs 'a startling note of absolute modernity.'[23] Both Whistler and Wilde were excluded from *The Yellow Book*'s pages, lest they monopolize publicity. Wilde pronounced it 'a great failure. I am so glad',[24] but could not evade association: many saw it as the creature of his countercultural wit.

Briefly, Beardsley turned to oil painting (45–46), inspired by the work of the seventeenth-century Spanish artist Diego Velázquez, which was on show in London. In other circumstances, he might have transitioned to the more prestigious medium. But the physical demands of easel painting, and the volatile oils and varnishes involved, were bad for his impaired lungs, even if his talents and techniques had not been so fully deployed in illustration; in the 1890s, although this might not have been the 'highest' medium, it certainly had star status. A satirical verse in *Punch* proclaimed:

> Take a lot of black triangles,
> Some amorphous blobs of red;
> Just a sprinkling of queer spangles,
> An ill-drawn Medusa head.[25]

Interviewed, Beardsley claimed prodigy status, declaring that his artistic mode was entirely personal. People 'appear differently to me than they do to others; to me they are mostly grotesque and I represent them as I see them', he said. 'Surely it is not my fault if they fall into certain lines and angles.'[26] He implied, too, that the designs were effortless, and always completed by candlelight in almost mystic seclusion. In fact, and thankfully, they were carefully crafted. As Robert Ross later wrote:

> He sketched everything in pencil, at first covering the paper with apparent scrawls, constantly rubbed out and blocked in again, until the whole surface became raddled from pencil, india rubber, and knife; over this incoherent surface he worked in Chinese ink with a gold pen, often ignoring the pencil lines, afterwards carefully removed. So every drawing was invented, built up, and completed on the same sheet of paper. And the same process was repeated even when he produced replicas.[27]

Their arresting qualities include the diversity of composition within the vertical format imposed by the printed page, and the enigmatic atmosphere conveyed in many images, like frames from a film. The first moving pictures – silent, monochrome, very short – coincided with Beardsley's output, and often portray similar effects of momentary glimpse and fleeting expression.

New projects and sexuality

A season of acclaim was, however, followed by a reverse. Aubrey and Mabel were at the premiere of Oscar Wilde's *The Importance of Being Earnest* in February 1895 when the Marquess of Queensberry (father of Lord Alfred Douglas, Wilde's devoted favourite) was barred from the theatre. Soon afterwards Queensberry challenged Wilde as a 'somdomite [*sic*]', and was sued for libel, but on acquittal provided witnesses to testify against Wilde in a criminal trial for gross indecency – that is, sex with other men. Wilde was arrested in April 1895 while carrying – perhaps deliberately – a yellow-covered novel, which was immediately misidentified as *The Yellow Book*. A moral panic ensued. Several eminent authors demanded that the publisher withdraw all Beardsley's designs. He was summarily dismissed as art editor. Mabel recalled this as bitterly humiliating. She and Aubrey moved to cheaper lodgings.

Contemporaries looked on with dismay. 'Damned young fool', observed Burne-Jones: '[H]e got onto all that horrid set of semi-sodomites, and after Oscar Wilde's disappearance had almost to disappear himself. ... In one season he was suddenly marched into that ridiculous position of his that was entirely invented by the critics, and he believed it.'[28]

Yet, as the poet William Butler Yeats later declared, 'being all young, we delighted in enemies',[29] and Beardsley would have concurred. Although his health worsened, he turned to new pictorial projects of his own choosing. These included an elaborate retelling of the Tannhäuser legend – already reworked by Wagner from the old German romance of the Venusberg – with equally elaborate illustrations in rococo mode (50). 'I am just doing a picture of Venus feeding her pet unicorns which have garlands of roses about their necks,' he told Frederick Evans.[30] He acquired new patrons, one being André Raffalovich (fig. 11), French-born poet and writer on homosexual 'inversion', and another Leonard Smithers, a lawyer-turned-bookseller with a special interest in classical pornography.

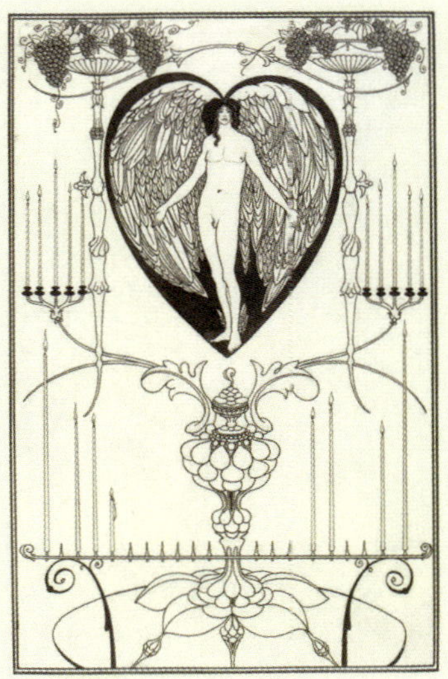

Fig. 11 *Mirror of Love*, design for the frontispiece for *The Thread and the Path* by Marc André Raffalovich, rejected by publisher David Nutt, 1895
Pen and ink over traces of graphite on paper
Victoria and Albert Museum, London (V&A: 1377-1931)

Both topics were of the age. Sexual orientation had become a subject of sociological enquiry along with the male taste for lewd or simply explicit stories in Greek, Latin and Arabic literature, which had hitherto been bowdlerized or kept from female readers. For Decadents, both were sticks with which to disgust the bourgeois and affirm their freedom from prudish convention. Beardsley frequently boasted of the indecency of his images.

Owing to the company he kept, his own sexuality has been much pondered, like that of his contemporary, the novelist Henry James. His dandy's attire, literary and theatrical tastes and socio-aesthetic friendships in the context of 1890s culture all suggest a gay identity that remains unconfirmed and indeed doubtful. Though his aesthete's pose was genuine, his style seems not to have been what was later called 'camp'. W.B. Yeats recalled him with a hangover contemplating his reflection in a mirror and saying 'Yes, yes, I look like a sodomite. But no, I am not that', and was himself convinced that Beardsley had 'no sexual abnormality'.[31] Homosexual acts, in public or private, were of course illegal, as Wilde's conviction demonstrated, but Beardsley's assertion about himself was surely accurate. Moreover, several factors, including the fastidious reticence that dandyism helped both to mask and to express, and above all the damaged lungs that prevented physical exertion, ruled out most sexual activity.

On at least one occasion, writing to Smithers while working on a design, he exclaimed 'there, I've given myself a cockstand! Still!'[32] Wilde acutely noted the affinity of Beardsley's images to 'the naughty scribbles [of] a precocious boy',[33] and the monstrous erections he drew in Aristophanes' *Lysistrata* (see p. 31) are certainly reminiscent of the long tradition of such scrawls on walls and toilet doors. Whether or not the drawings were arousing, they certainly still appear shocking and obscene. Using Victorian pornography as a yardstick, Burne-Jones found Beardsley's works 'detestable ... more lustful than any I've seen – not that I've seen many such. There was a woman with breasts each larger than her head, which was quite tiny and features insignificant, so that she looked like a mere lustful animal.'[34]

The Savoy

Smithers offered to support a successor-rival to *The Yellow Book*, under the joint editorship of Beardsley and Arthur Symons, who admired the French poets Baudelaire and Verlaine and had written on the Symbolist movement in literature. At Dieppe in late summer 1895, plans for *The Savoy* were laid (fig. 12). 'He had that absorption of a lifetime in an hour which we find in those who hasten to have done their work before noon, knowing that they will not see the evening,' wrote Symons.[35] Beardsley was just 23; characteristically, he envisaged new directions, notably as author as well as illustrator, and inspired by eighteenth-century French artists and writers like Antoine Watteau and Pierre Choderlos de

Fig. 12 Cover of *The Savoy*, no. 2 (April 1896)
Line block print
Victoria and Albert Museum, London (V&A: E.367-1899)

THE SAVOY

AN ILLUSTRATED QUARTERLY

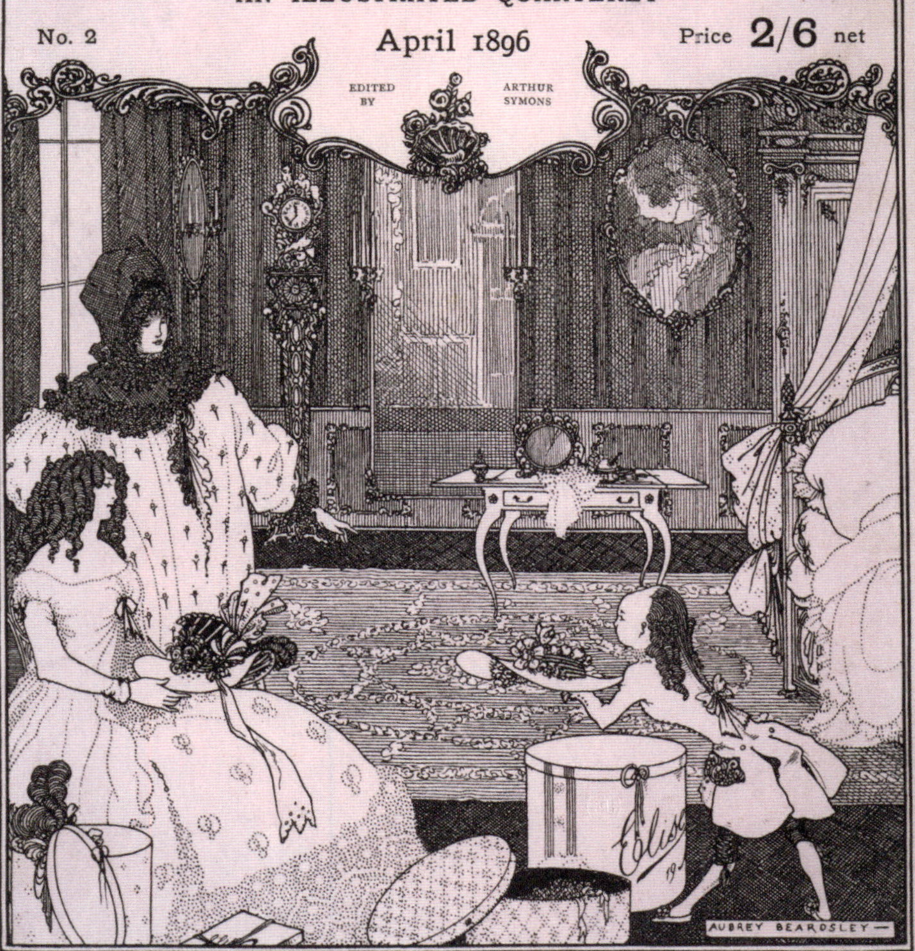

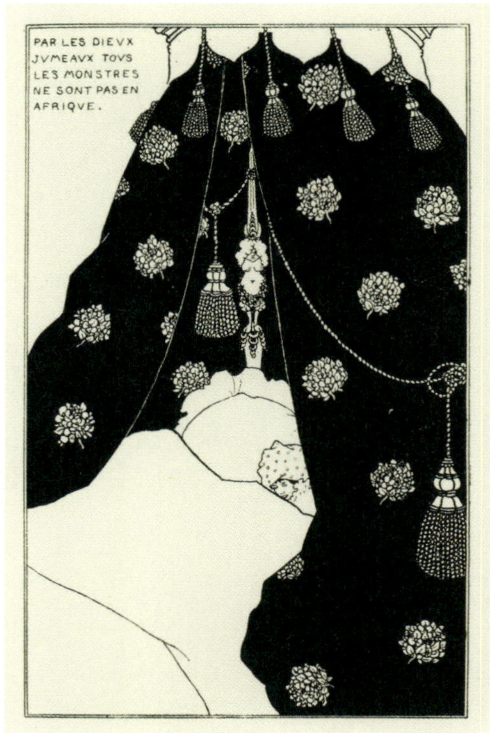

Fig. 13 *Self-portrait in bed*,
by Aubrey Beardsley, 1894
Line block print
Victoria and Albert Museum, London
(V&A: E.429-1899)

Laclos. His imagination bounded forward, possibly because every pulmonary haemorrhage threatened to shorten his life. Enforced rest stimulated more and more ideas (47–52).

His new pictorial style flourished in illustrations to Pope's mock-heroic poem *The Rape of the Lock* (61–67), which feature eighteenth-century fashions – panniered skirts and high head-pieces adorned with ribbons and lace for women, and embroidered coats and high heels for men. In place of the dramatic contrasts of black and white, these designs are abundantly over-wrought, all-over patterned, and confusingly crammed with intricately prinked, pricked, hatched detail, in a manner that exceeds the gracious engraving of the Neoclassical age. The severity of line gives way to a filigree of dancing dots and curlicues. Whistler, surprised by the change, declared his support, saying 'Aubrey, I have made a very great mistake – you are a very great artist.'[36] The other great change in Beardsley's life, also probably prompted by awareness of his mortality, was his move towards the spiritual comforts of Catholicism, whither Mabel had led the way. In part another manifestation of perversity, this chimed with fashionable crazes for the occult and mystical that were akin to the adoption of 'Eastern' religion in the hippie culture of the later 1960s. But it also marked Beardsley's sense of self-knowledge and quest for much-needed consolation, while at the same time assisting his chameleon tendencies, presenting different masks to each acquaintance while reserving a camouflaged self – or, perhaps, the masks were the self.

According to Yeats, Aubrey was 'not loveable, only astounding and intrepid'.[37] Despite public nonchalance, he was also a very frightened young man with a fatal condition. Beardsley had spent all his adult life as an invalid, frequently bed-bound. A self-portrait of the artist in bed shows a tiny figure beneath a large, tasselled canopy and pole decorated with phallic symbols, cowering from nightmares (fig. 13). 'Not all monsters are in Africa' proclaims the gnomic inscription, swearing by 'the twin gods', who may be Castor and Pollux or Hypnos (Sleep) and Thanatos (Death).

Away from religion, when Smithers proposed an illustrated version of Aristophanes' comedy *Lysistrata*, about an anti-war 'sex strike' by Greek women, which would evade prosecution for obscenity if sold 'privately' rather than through the book trade, Beardsley seized on the idea. He produced a sequence of outrageous images (54–60) depicting sexual frustration in both sexes and featuring especially outsize, elegantly outlined penises. Copied from erotic Japanese prints, these must have shocked and excited his (male) audience and identified his art as no longer 'weird' but salacious. In other respects, the drawings returned to the outline mode, chiefly blank with black passages; male and female figures wear the feathered hats and garter stockings of cabaret dancers. They have been described as exhibiting a 'pagan frankness' distinct from contemporary voyeurism,[38] and are indeed masterworks of comic art. 'Beardsley was one of the first artists to confront sexuality head on,' Stephen Calloway has declared:

> The closest recent parallel, I suppose, is Robert Mapplethorpe, in the way he uses absolutely explicit imagery in a rather cool manner. They're both masters of black and white and share a similar temperament, that dispassionate way of producing things which are actually extremely outrageous. And the fact that they both died young has a curious new resonance.[39]

Fig. 14 *Juvenal scourging Woman*, by Aubrey Beardsley, frontispiece to the *Sixth Satire* of Juvenal, in *An Issue of Five Drawings Illustrative of Juvenal and Lucian*, published by Leonard Smithers, London, 1906
Line block print
Victoria and Albert Museum, London (V&A: E.683-1945)

After serious sickness in Brussels in spring 1896, Beardsley's life was reduced to invalidism. Unable to travel unaided or climb stairs without coughing blood, he was confined to beds and sofas and on medical advice banished from London's polluted atmosphere. In Epsom, Surrey, he drew the *Lysistrata* illustrations; as his school education would not have given him deep skills in ancient Greek, he worked from the French version by Maurice Donnay, which had been performed in Paris with the celebrated actress Réjane in the title role.[40] Aristophanes was succeeded by the Roman satirist Juvenal (fig. 14, 68–71) – Beardsley had better knowledge of Latin than Greek – and Epsom was succeeded by Boscombe, Hampshire, outside Bournemouth.

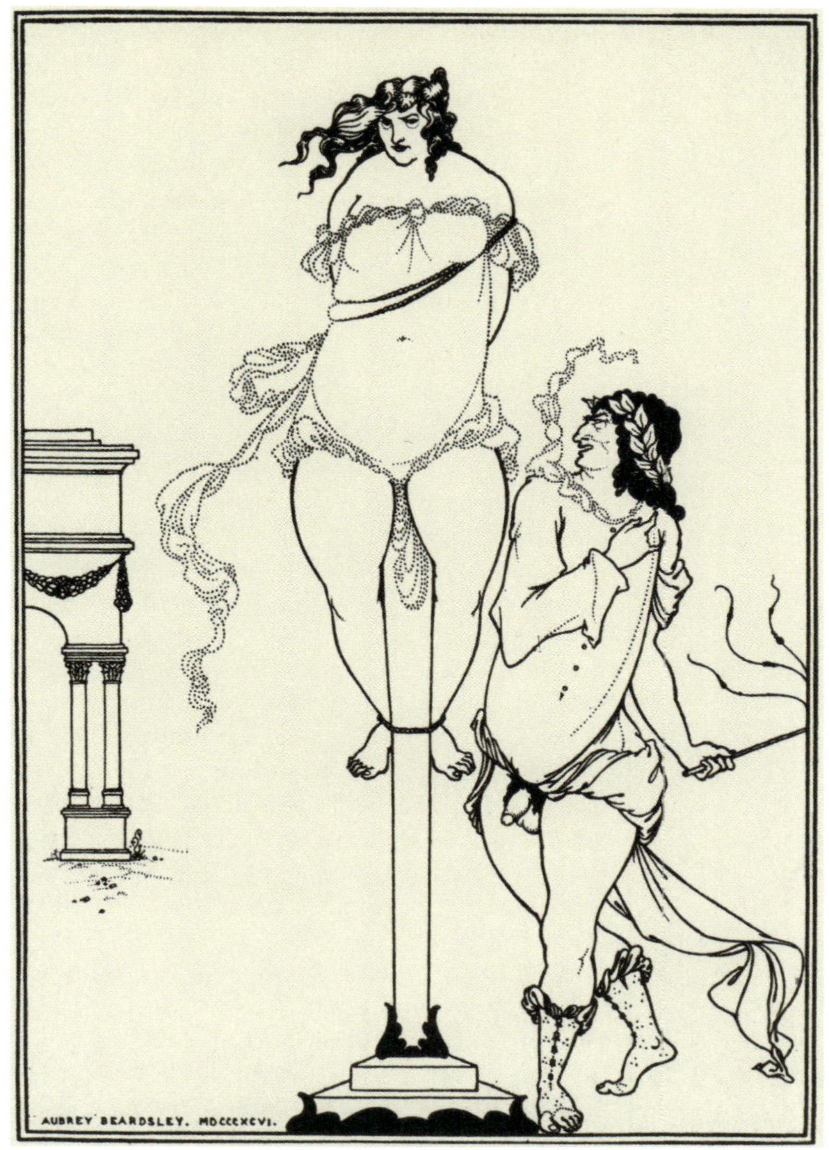
AUBREY BEARDSLEY. MDCCCXCVI.

Last illustrations and death

On a short trip to London, Beardsley answered one polite greeting with 'I'm at death's door, but that's no matter.'[41] Foreknowledge, however, prompted Smithers to propose an 'album' of 50 drawings, essentially as a memorial volume. Beardsley was energized, if only graphically, returning to Wagner with illustrations to *Das Rheingold*. Alberich, he contended, was the original form of the name Aubrey. Next came the famous cross-dressing Mademoiselle de Maupin (fig. 15), cast as a fictional heroine by Théophile Gautier in what became a sourcebook of gender fluidity for the Aesthetic movement (72–73). Beardsley bought watercolour paints, thinking to add tints to his delicate grotesqueries. He also agreed to switch to half-tone printing. *The Savoy* folded. Mabel departed on a theatre company tour of North America. In March 1897 Aubrey joined the Catholic Church. Escorted by his mother and a doctor, he travelled to Paris and then to Dieppe; fortuitously Wilde was also staying nearby, under the post-imprisonment name of Sebastian Melmoth. They went shopping together, when Wilde persuaded Beardsley to buy a silver-grey top hat.

In the autumn he moved to Menton on the French Riviera and started work on a new project, illustrating the Jacobean drama *Volpone*, by Ben Jonson, about a monstrous miser. Volpone was 'a splendid sinner', he wrote, who compelled 'admiration by the fineness and very excess of his wickedness … we are scarcely shocked by his lust, so magnificent is the vehemence of his passion, and we marvel and are aghast rather than disgusted by his cunning and audacity.'[42] Greed, deception and the shameless pursuit of wealth were aspects that many saw in late Victorian plutocracy, as capitalist competition fuelled the Western world. Beardsley's drawings – a title page and five initials, mostly elaborate Vs (74) – kept to the Jacobean period, however, with baroque jewels, a satyr, an elephant, a buxom Venus and a chubby Cupid, all imbued with sinister energy. The book, he declared with deathbed ambition, would be in his new 'grand style', a compelling example of graphic imagination.

Aubrey Beardsley died in Menton on 16 March 1898, aged 25, with many such projects unfulfilled. Friends and followers mourned the premature loss of such skill, invention and creative energy that would surely have continued to startle, delight and confound viewers, had he lived.

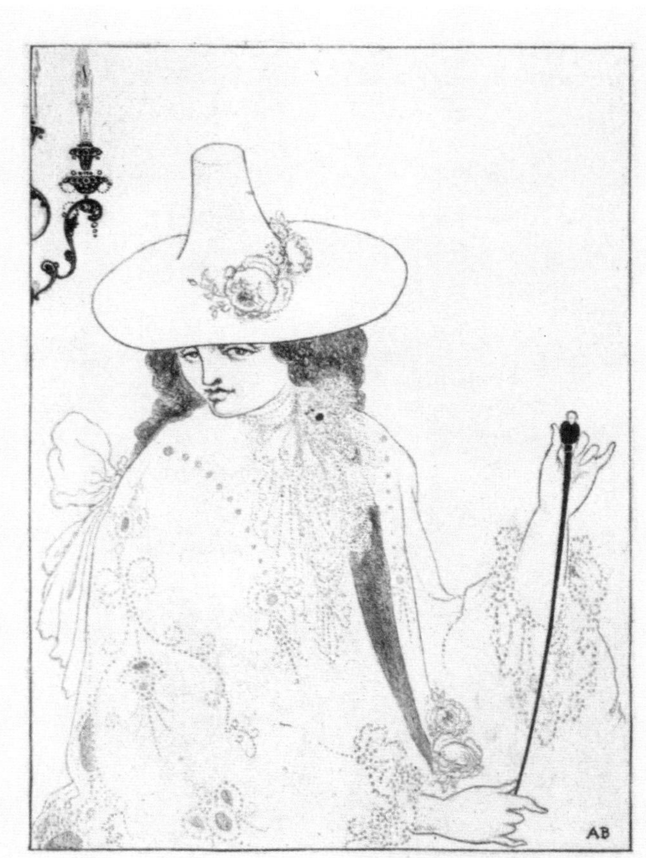

Fig. 15. *D'Albert*, a vignette from *Mademoiselle de Maupin*, 1897
Photogravure on paper
Victoria and Albert Museum, London
(V&A: E.417-1972)

Plates

Beardsley was 'particularly proud' of this slightly mysterious, slightly melancholic study of a country girl.[43] The visual balance of figure and pitchfork foreshadows later compositions, giving an impressionistic, *plein-air* effect. The title on an autograph copy[44] links it to a drama starring Sarah Bernhardt performed in London in June 1890, but here Joan of Arc is working in the fields where she experienced her visions.

1. *Jeanne d'Arc*, *c.*1890
Ink and wash on paper
Victoria and Albert Museum, London
(V&A: E.18-1900)

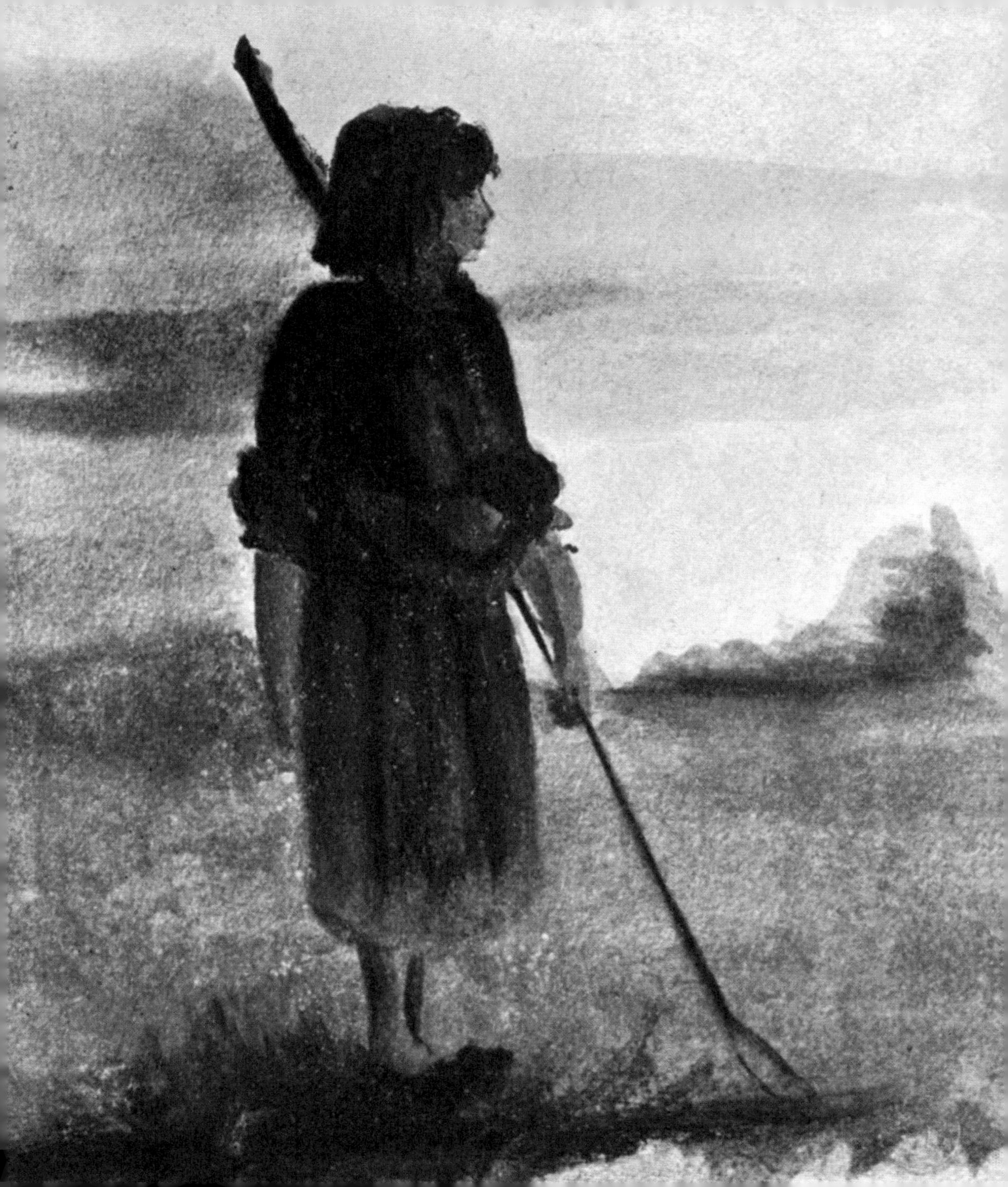

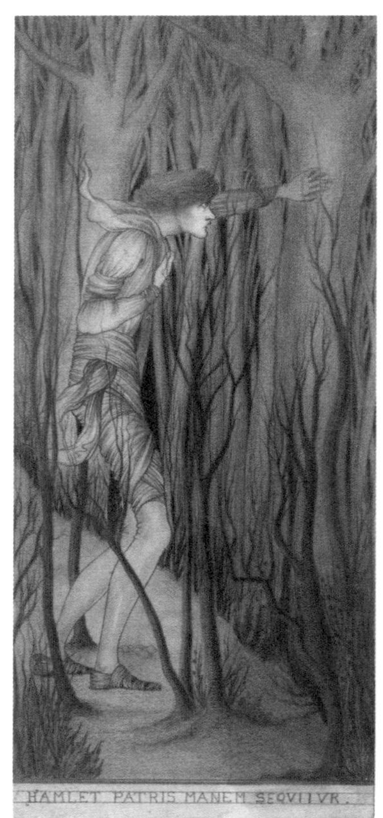

2. *Hamlet following the Ghost of his Father*, 1892–3
Graphite (pencil) on paper
British Museum
(BM: 1922,1209.8)

Aptly emblematic of an innovative yet inexperienced artist, this atmospheric image echoes figures and forests in Edward Burne-Jones's *Briar Rose* series (1890). Shakespeare's hero is shown as an etiolated youth at the edge of a dense wood, whose quest seems to reflect the feeble presence of the artist's bankrupt father within the household. The drawing was commissioned by Beardsley's former housemaster at Brighton Grammar School.[45]

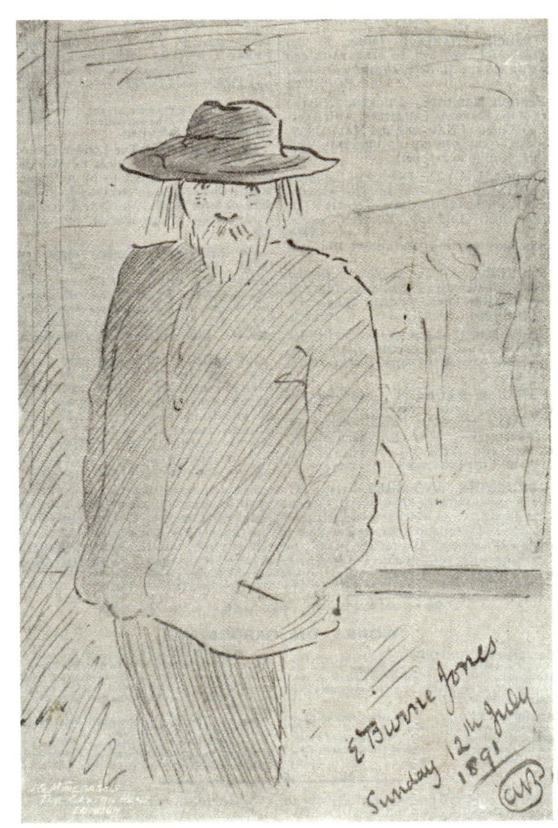

3. Sketch of Edward Burne-Jones, 12 July 1891
Half-tone print
Victoria and Albert Museum, London
(V&A: E.20-1900)

'There is *no* doubt about your gift,' Burne-Jones told Beardsley when they first met in July 1891; 'I *seldom* or *never* advise anyone to take up art as a profession, but in *your* case *I can do nothing else.*' This, as Beardsley reported, 'from the greatest living artist in Europe. Afterwards we returned to the lawn and had afternoon tea. Mrs Burne-Jones is very charming.'[46] The sketch was done the same day, from memory.

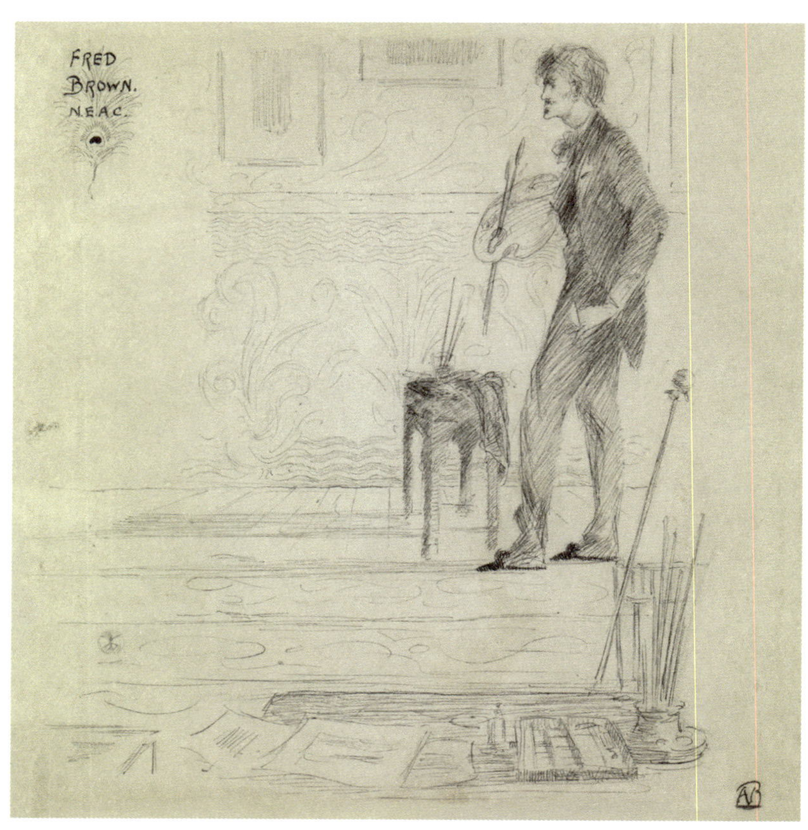

4. *Professor Fred Brown*, 1892
Pencil and ink on paper
Tate
(N04235)

Frederick Brown was principal of Westminster School of Art when Beardsley studied there; Beardsley made swift charcoal studies from plaster casts before joining the life class. Exacting but encouraging, Brown recommended his pupil to exhibit with the New English Art Club, where one review noted his 'freakish talent', power of design and 'technical resources in fine line and rich blacks'.[47]

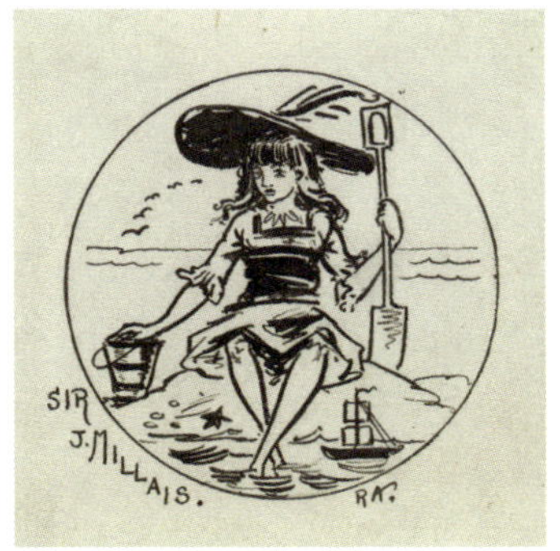

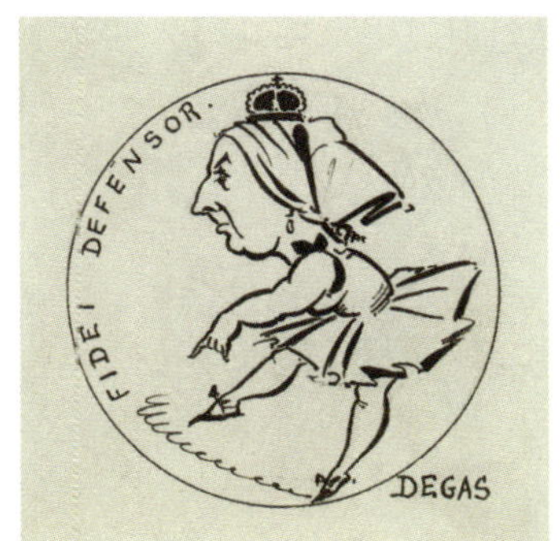

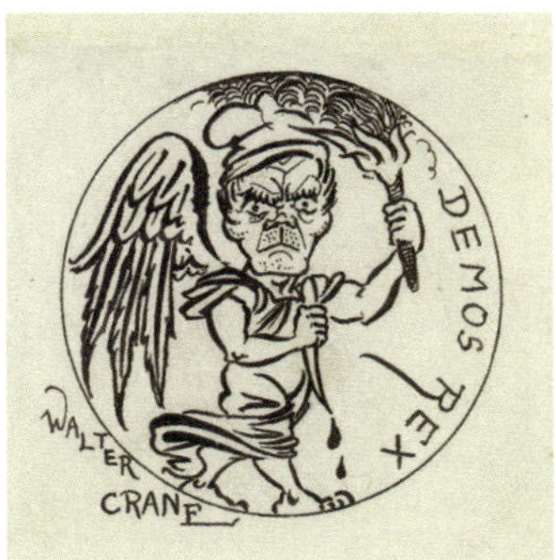

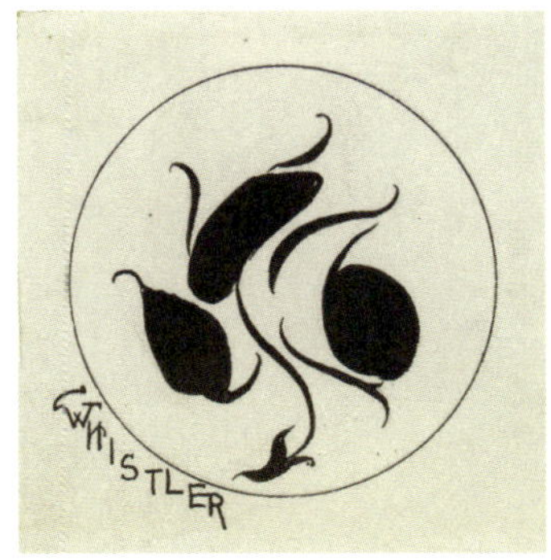

5. *The New Coinage*, 1893
Pen, ink and graphite on paper
Victoria and Albert Museum, London
(V&A: E.36 to 39-1948)
Bequeathed by H.H. Harrod

These pictorial satires on the redesigned British coins were drawn for a weekly newspaper. Described as 'not sent in for competition', Beardsley's comic designs included Britannia as if by John Everett Millais; Queen Victoria as a Degas dancer; a republican socialist worker as if by Walter Crane; and a floral emblem in the egocentric manner of J.A.M. Whistler's signature. The image of Victoria was deemed too provocative even as a parody, and was suppressed.

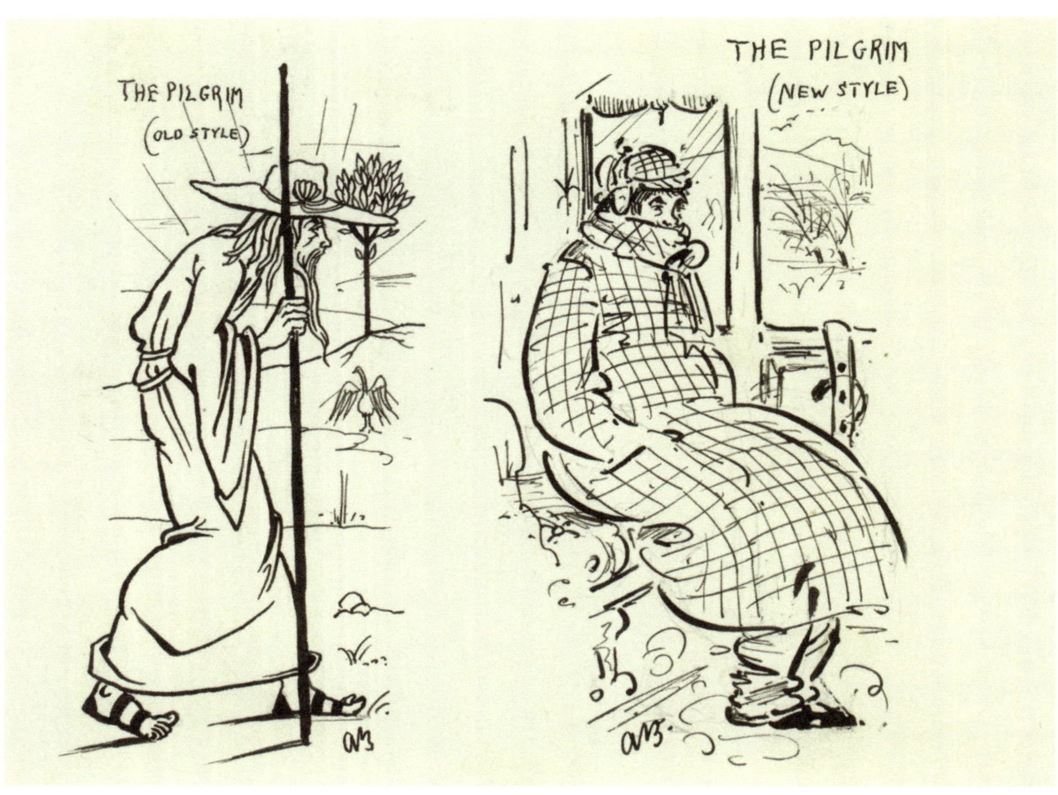

6. *Pope Leo XIII's Jubilee. The Pilgrim (old style). The Pilgrim (new style)*, drawing for an illustration in the *Pall Mall Budget*, 23 February 1893, p. 270
Pen and ink over pencil on paper
Victoria and Albert Museum, London
(V&A: E.334-1972)

This is another contemporary satire, on the 500 British pilgrims, led by the Duke of Norfolk, heading for Rome to mark the jubilee of Pope Leo XIII. Their names were published on 4 February 1893. The 'unqualified success' of the mission, despite a rough Channel crossing and a 'hurried but far from rapid rail journey', was reported on 11 March.[48]

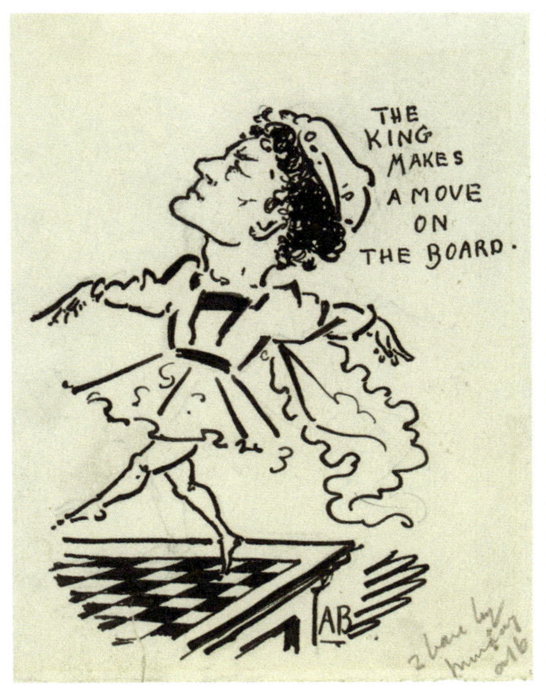

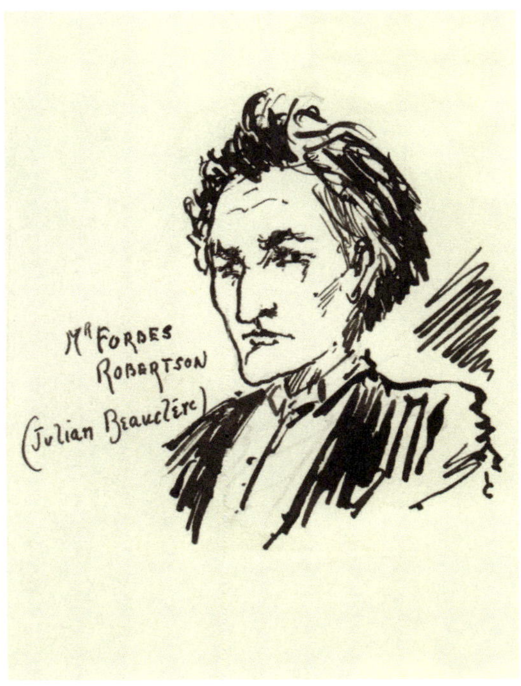

7. *Mr Forbes-Robertson (Julian Beauclerc)* and *The King Makes a Move on the Board*, two caricatures of actors in character, 1893
Pen and ink on paper
Victoria and Albert Museum, London
(V&A: E31 to 32-1948)
Bequeathed by H.H. Harrod

The two actors depicted on the London stage in these sketches are Johnston Forbes-Robertson as Julian Beauclerc in *Diplomacy* at the Garrick Theatre and William Terriss as Henry II in Alfred, Lord Tennyson's *Becket* at the Lyceum. They were two of the leading actors of the time, although both were overshadowed by Henry Irving. The 1890s was a decade of spectacular staging and Beardsley was an eager theatre-goer with a keen eye and swift pen. His sister, Mabel, acted in supporting ingénue roles.

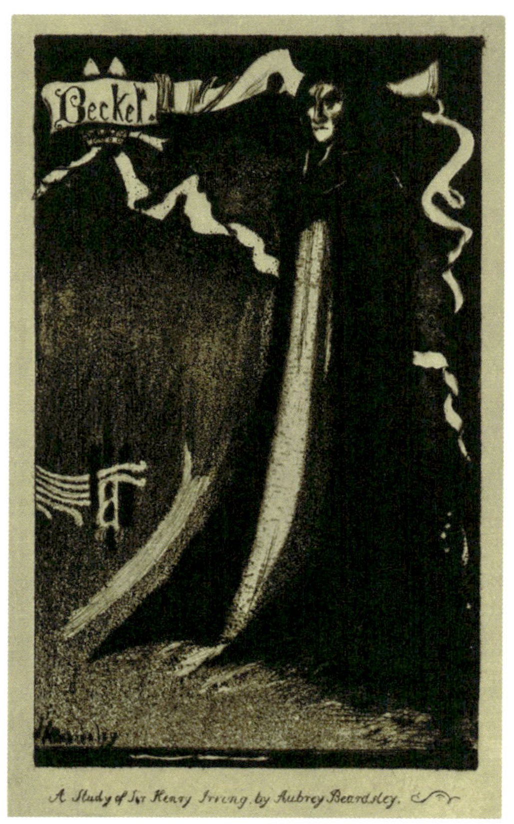

8. *Henry Irving as Thomas a'Becket*, 1893
Drypoint and aquatint print on paper
British Museum
(BM: 1960,0409.502)

The star performance of the 1893 winter season in London was Sir Henry Irving in the title role of Tennyson's *Becket* at the Lyceum Theatre. With a weekly commission from the *Pall Mall Budget*, Beardsley aimed to 'make the old black-and-white duffers sit up'. Although this cover design betrays his inexperience with drypoint etching and aquatint and was not admired, it signals his emerging skill with dramatic dark forms.

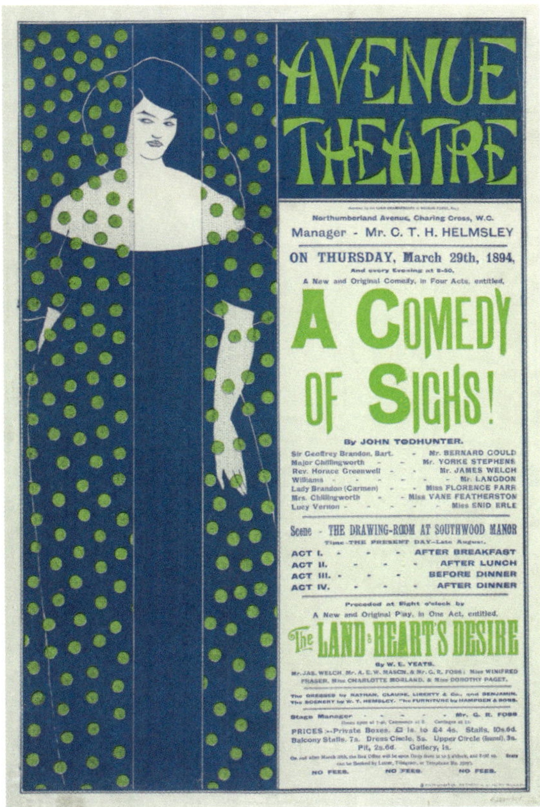

9. *A Comedy of Sighs*, theatre poster advertising two productions at the Avenue Theatre, London, 29 March 1894
Colour lithograph
Victoria and Albert Museum, London (V&A: E.289-1925)
Given by Miss Gwen John

With developments in bold colour printing, a new spirit entered poster art in the 1890s, responding to work by Jules Chéret, Toulouse-Lautrec and Alphonse Mucha. This poster was commissioned by actor Florence Farr, who appeared in both advertised pieces. It announces both *A Comedy of Sighs* by John Todhunter and *The Land of Heart's Desire*, the first publicly performed play by W.B. Yeats, in which a mysterious child urges a new bride to escape to the land of faery.

Vignette from *Bon-Mots of Sydney Smith and R. Brinsley Sheridan*, edited by Walter Jerrold and published by J.M. Dent & Co., London, 1893, p. 177
Pen and ink on paper
Victoria and Albert Museum, London
(V&A: E.321-1972)

Bon-Mots (literally 'good words' but meaning 'witticisms') was a sequence of small books containing jokes and anecdotes from earlier writers, including humorist Sydney Smith (1771–1845), essayist Charles Lamb (1775–1834) and practical joker Theodore Hook (1788–1841). Borrowing liberally from comic dramatists Richard Brinsley Sheridan (1751–1816), Douglas Jerrold (1803–57) and Samuel Foote (1720–77), the humour resembles that of the magazine *Punch*. Beardsley produced 130 unrelated 'grotesques' or absurd designs, in keeping with the verbal drollery, to decorate the series. A selection of these are reproduced in this book in between the plate sections.

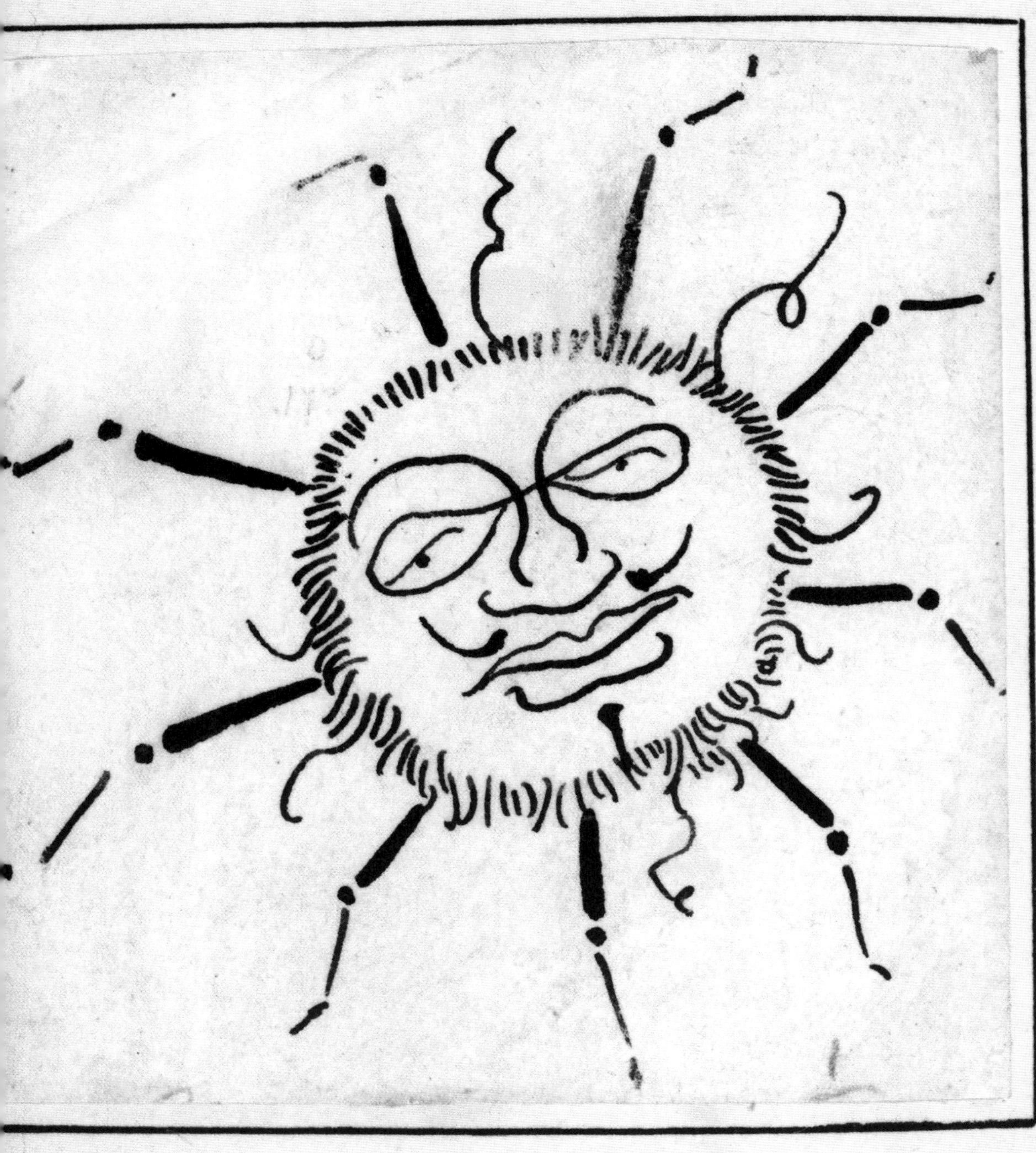

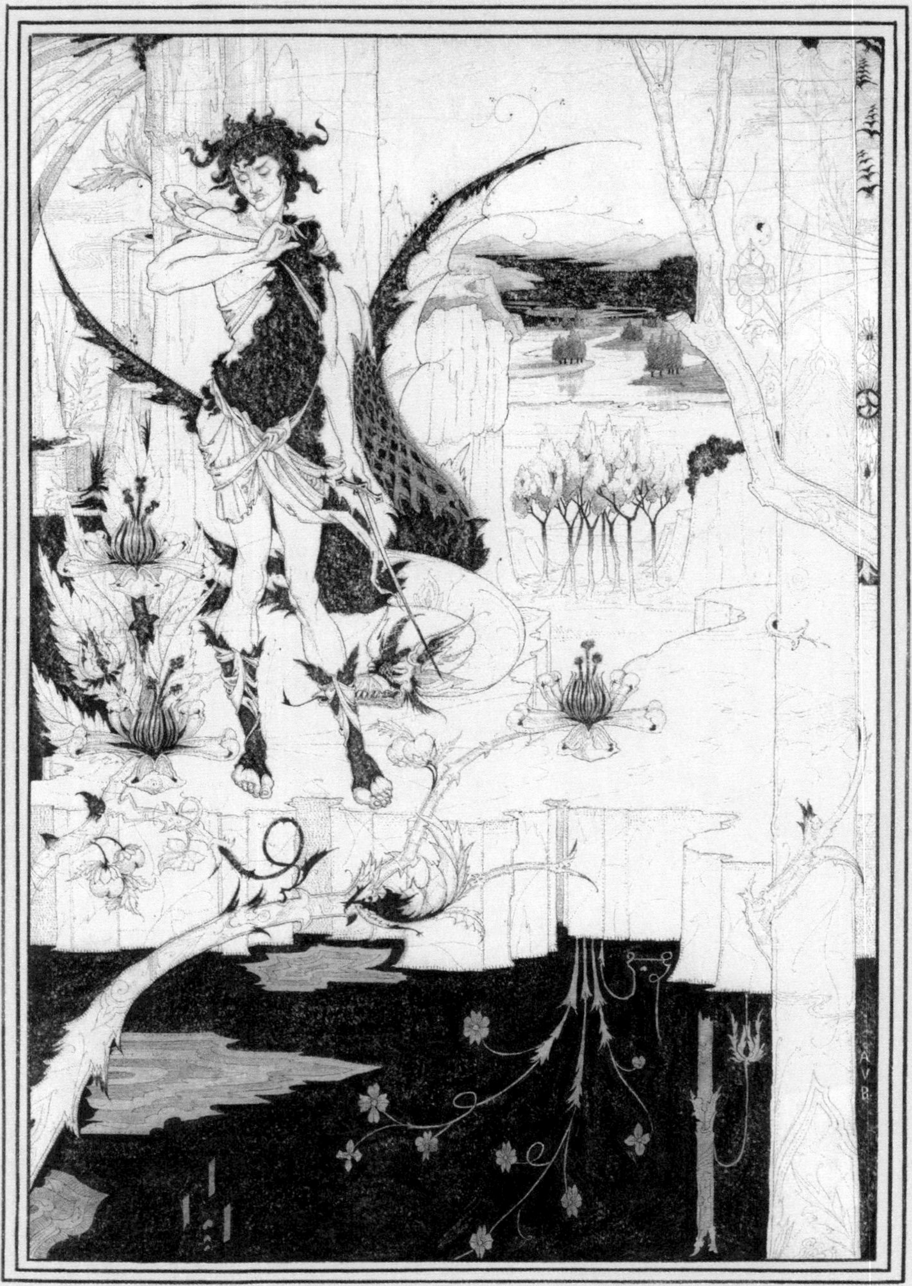
AVB

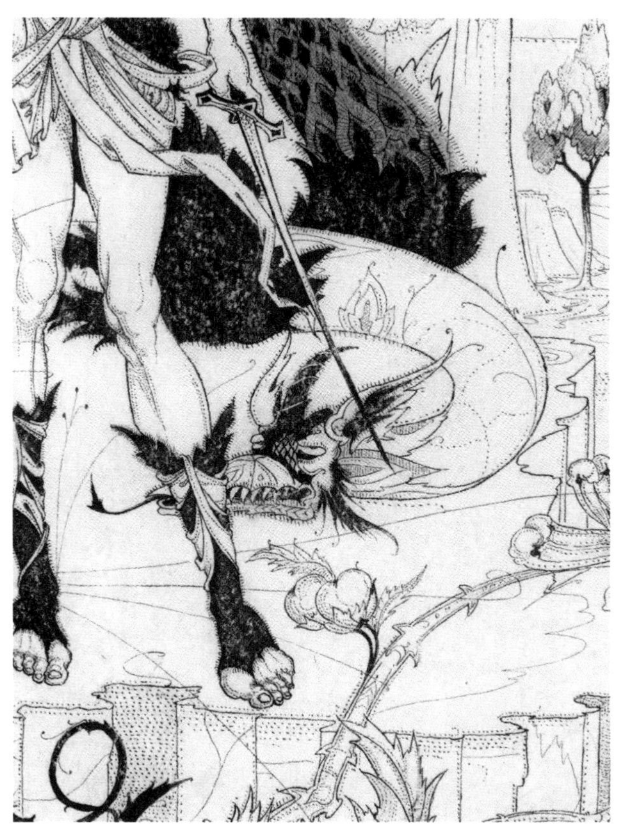

10. *Siegfried*, Act II, 1892–3
Pen, ink and wash on paper
Victoria and Albert Museum, London
(V&A: E.578-1932)

Responding to the vogue for Wagnerian opera, this drawing depicts the moment when Siegfried, having slain the dragon Fafnir, licks the creature's blood from his hand. Beardsley described the style of the design, with its intricate overlying hairline webs, as his 'entirely new method of drawing and composition'.[49] The hero's androgyncus pose is often cited as epitomizing Decadent sexuality and 'the neurosis of the age', with its 'delight in anything strange and depraved'.[50]

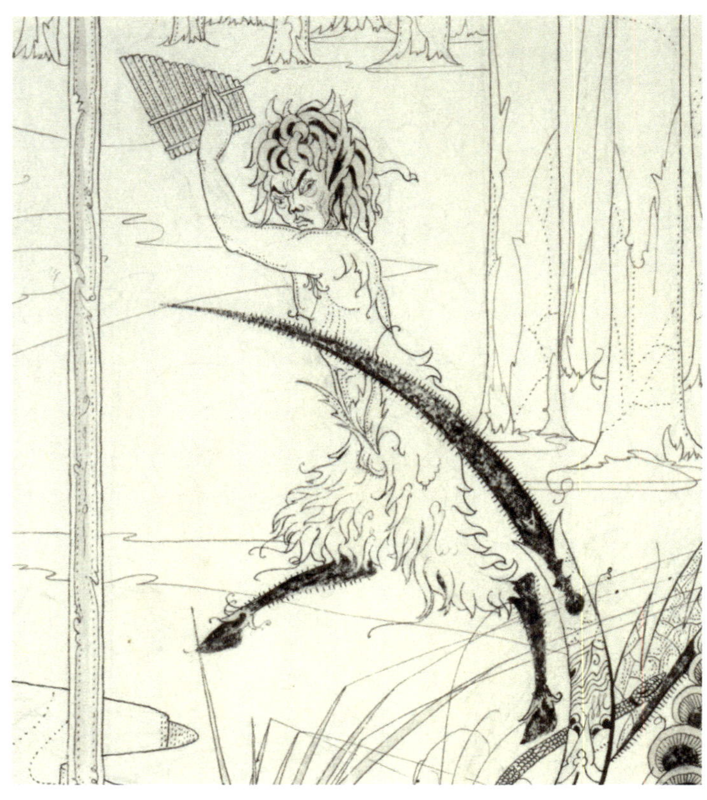

11. *How Arthur Saw the Questing Beast*, drawing for the photogravure frontispiece for *Le Morte Darthur by Thomas Malory*, vol. 1, published by J.M. Dent & Co., London, 1893
Pen, ink and wash on paper
Victoria and Albert Museum, London (V&A: E.289-1972)

In *Le Morte Darthur* – Thomas Malory's version of the legends of King Arthur – the 'Questing Beast', with snake's head, leopard's body and voice like baying hounds, was born from an incestuous union. King Arthur sees it after his affair with his half-sister. Beardsley chose this perverse and obscure episode from the legends for a companion image to *Siegfried* (10) and then made it the frontispiece of his own edition of the work. Typically, the images are decadent, beautiful and faithful to Malory's narrative.[51]

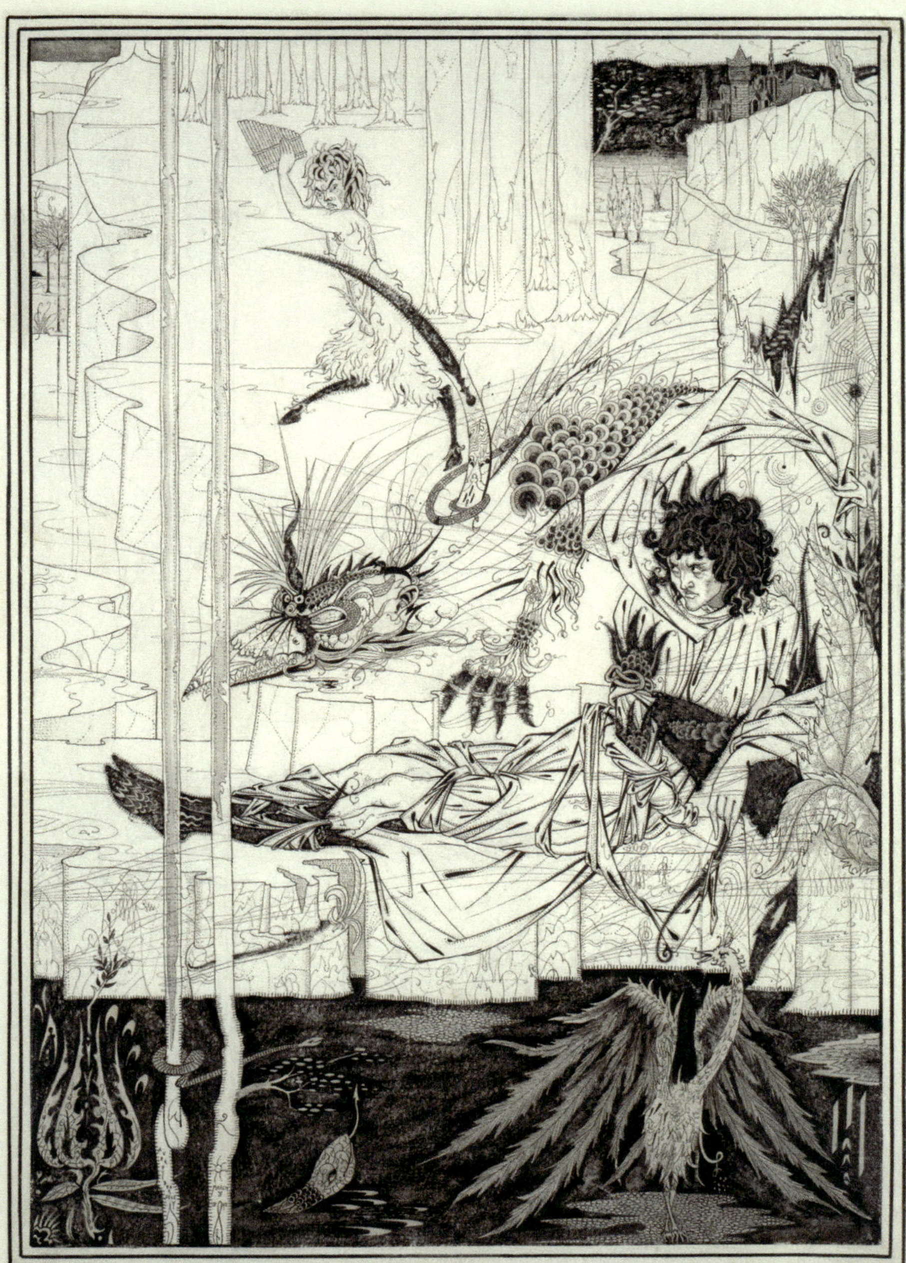

Beardsley described the subjects of this print as 'Quite mad and a little indecent'.[52] The frieze of comic male figures bearing gifts to an enthroned woman (who is named for a cicada) mixes influences from Japanese prints with those from ancient Greek vases. Criticized as an exercise in 'mocking diablerie',[53] it was published in the first number of *The Studio* in April 1893, together with *Siegfried* (10), *Les Revenants de Musique* and Beardsley's earliest *Salome* illustration, *J'ai baisé ta bouche Jokanaan.*

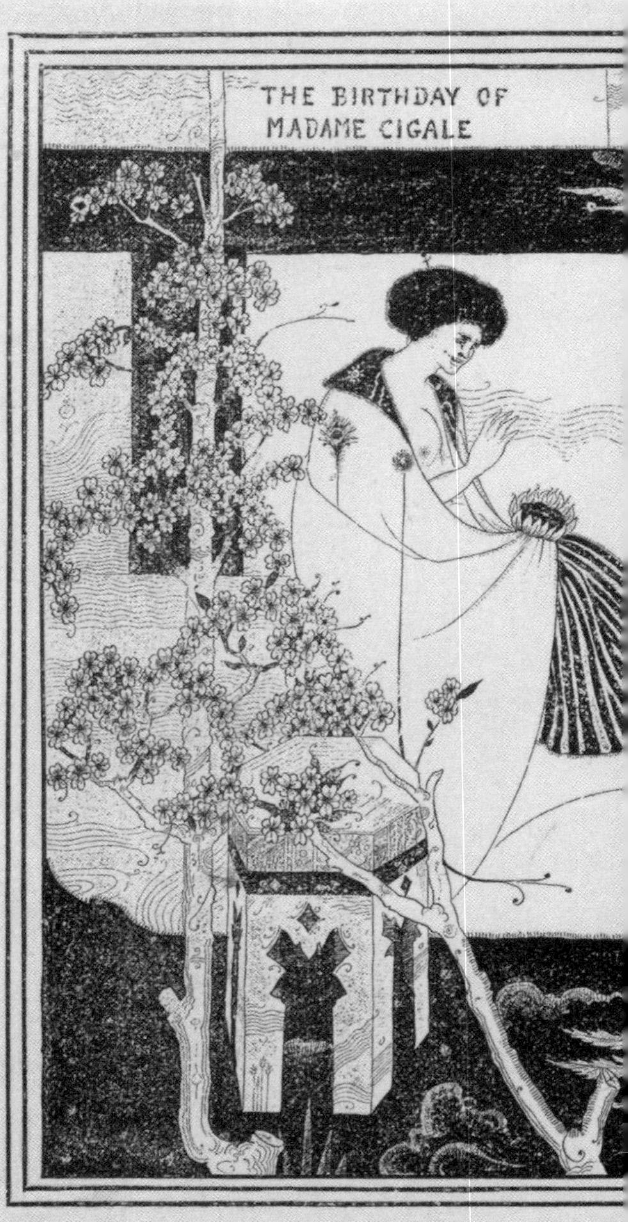

12. *The Birthday of Madame Cigale*, 1893
Line block print
Victoria and Albert Museum, London
(V&A: E.450-1899)

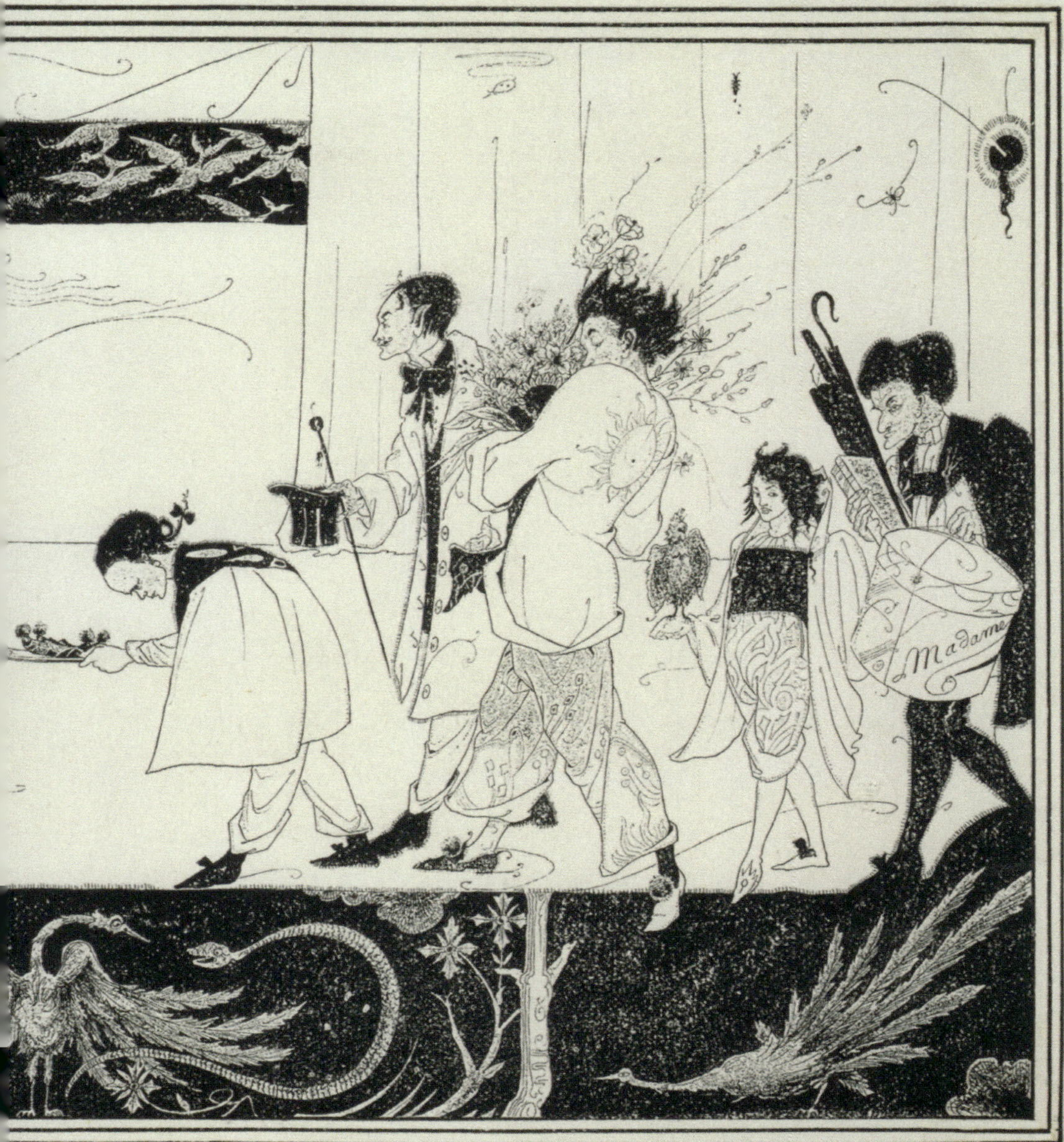
Madame

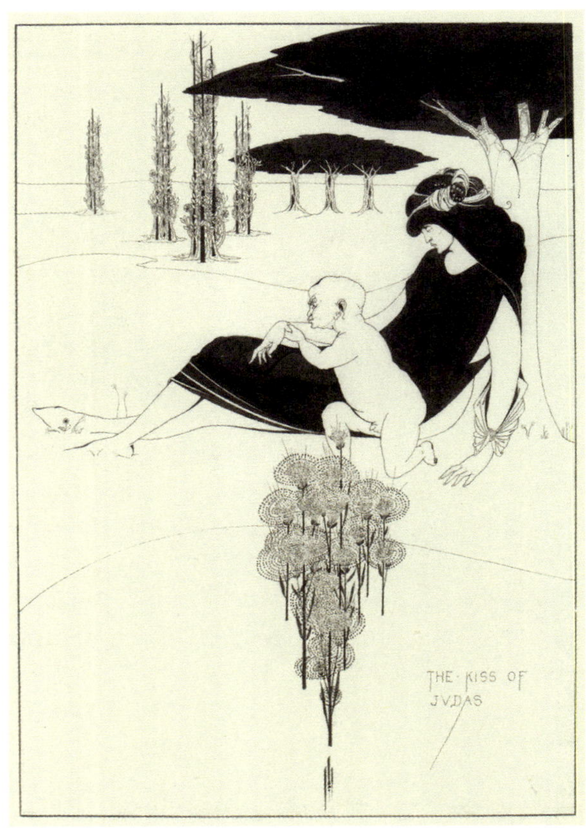

13. *The Kiss of Judas*, published in the *Pall Mall Magazine*, July 1893
Pen and ink on paper
Victoria and Albert Museum, London
(V&A: E.292-1972)

Commissioned to illustrate a macabre and 'awfully striking legend' that contained a 'strange form kissing its victim' together with other diabolical episodes, this was drawn for publication in the *Pall Mall Magazine*, while Beardsley was in Paris. 'I should like the broken effect of the Judas flowers to be kept', he told the editor.[54]

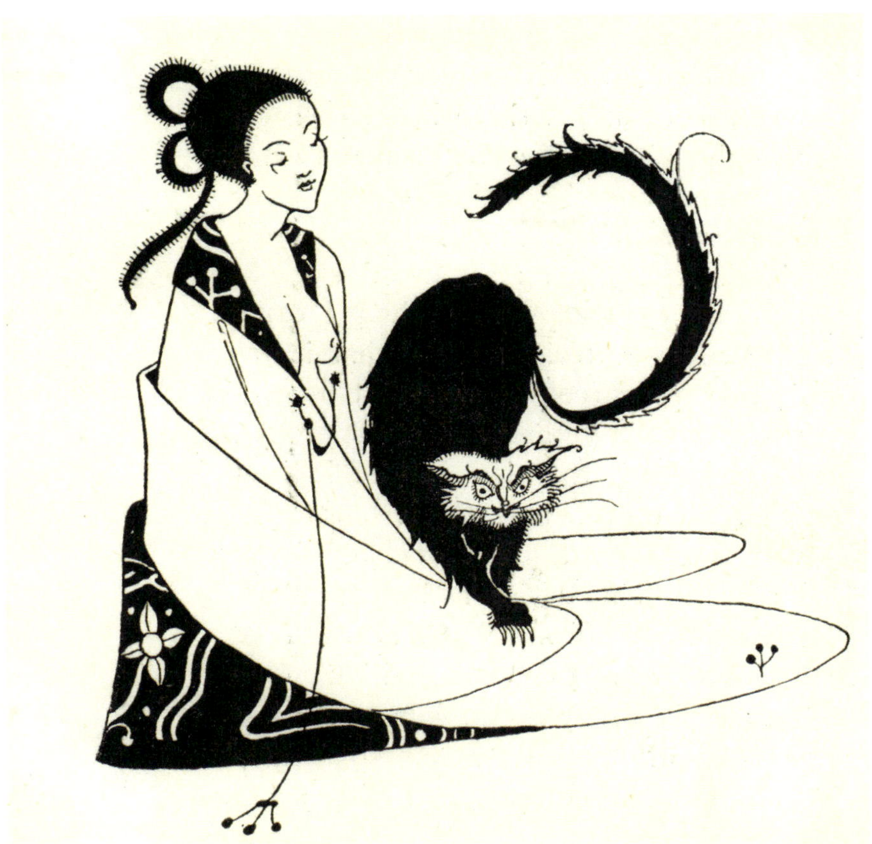

14. Vignette from *Bon-Mots of Sydney Smith and R. Brinsley Sheridan*, edited by Walter Jerrold and published by J.M. Dent & Co., London, 1893, p. 76
Line block print
Victoria and Albert Museum, London
(V&A: E.540-1899)

Japanese *shunga* prints introduced Beardsley to explicit erotic imagery and to woodblock printing with flat colour and highly patterned shapes. Cats also feature in many *shunga* scenes. Here the staring eyes and claws of the outsize feline with sinister yet comical tail are juxtaposed with a geisha, whose demure expression belies her dishabille, in an unsettling composition enfolded in graceful elliptical curves.

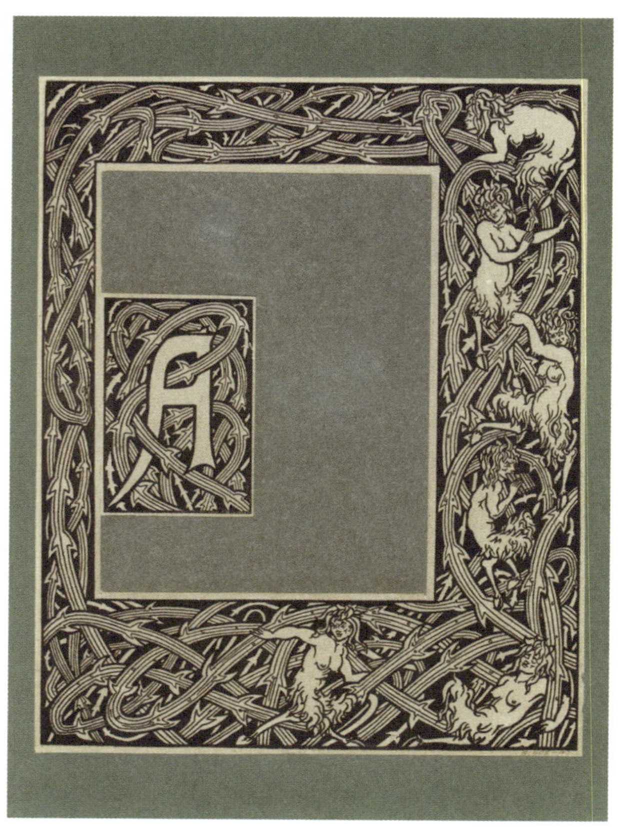

15. Design for *Le Morte Darthur* by Thomas Malory, published by J.M. Dent & Co., London, 1893–4
Line block print
Victoria and Albert Museum, London (V&A: E.405-1899)

An illustrated edition of Malory's tales of King Arthur and the Knights of the Round Table, the great late medieval sourcebook, was Beardsley's first major commission. The style followed the format designed by William Morris for the Kelmscott Press, with decorated initials and borders of sinister intertwining branches, here cheekily populated by hermaphrodite satyrs.

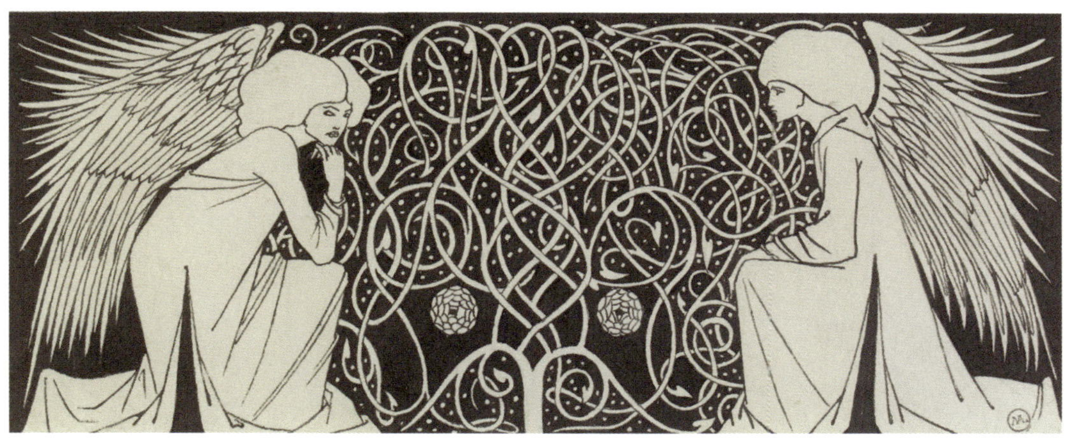

16. Ornamental design for
Le Morte Darthur by Thomas Malory,
published by J.M. Dent & Co.,
London, 1893–4
Pen and ink on paper
Victoria and Albert Museum, London
(V&A: D.1823-1904)

A pair of opposed angels kneel on either side of swirling Celtic interlace inspired by decorated manuscript gospels like those in the Book of Kells. The filigree white lines are patterned against black in best *fin de siècle* manner, with suitably androgynous figures. Within the horizontal space of the design, which resembles enamelled Arts and Crafts plaques, the asymmetrical, almost unruly elements are held in equilibrium by balance and repose.

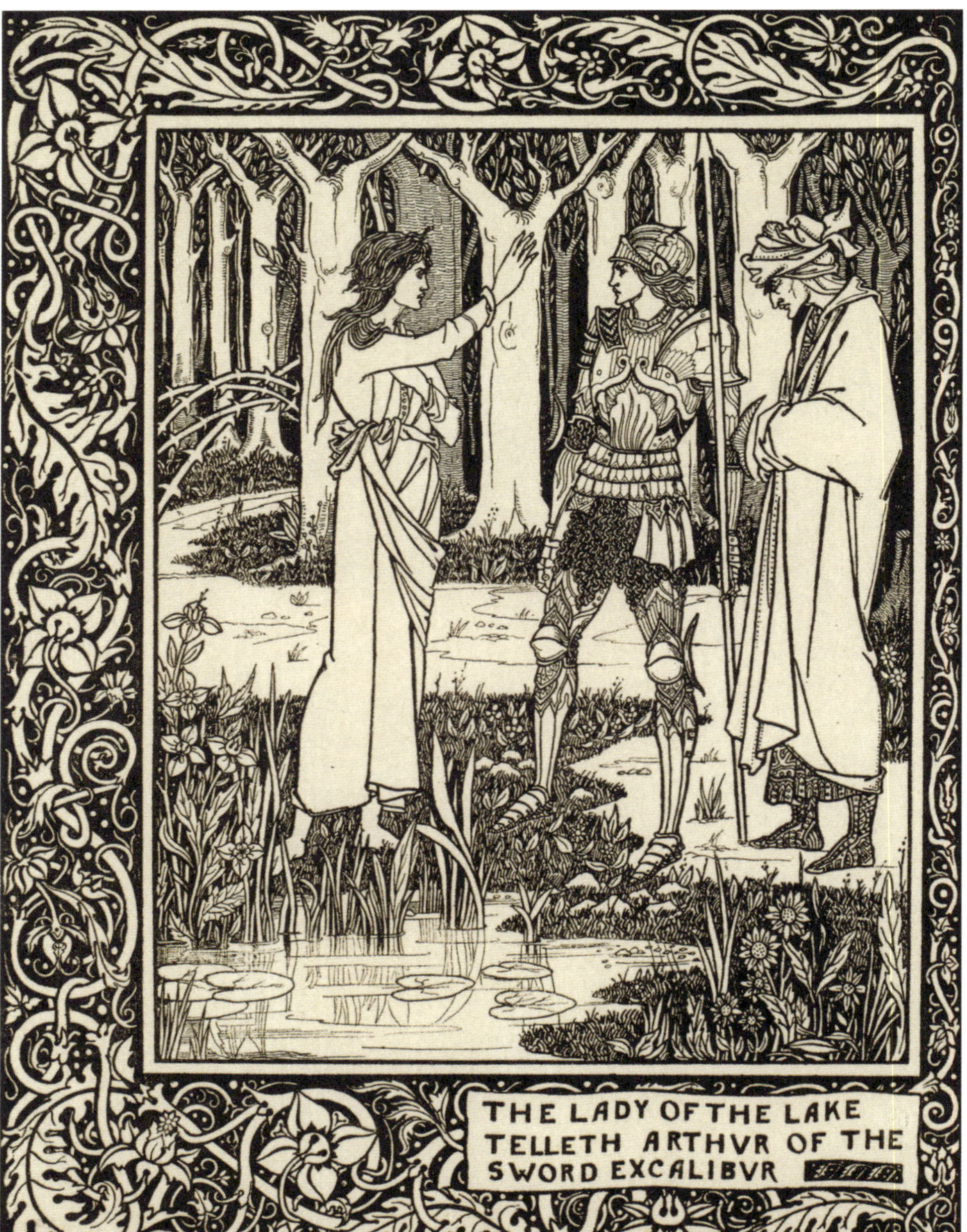
THE LADY OF THE LAKE
TELLETH ARTHVR OF THE
SWORD EXCALIBVR
AVB

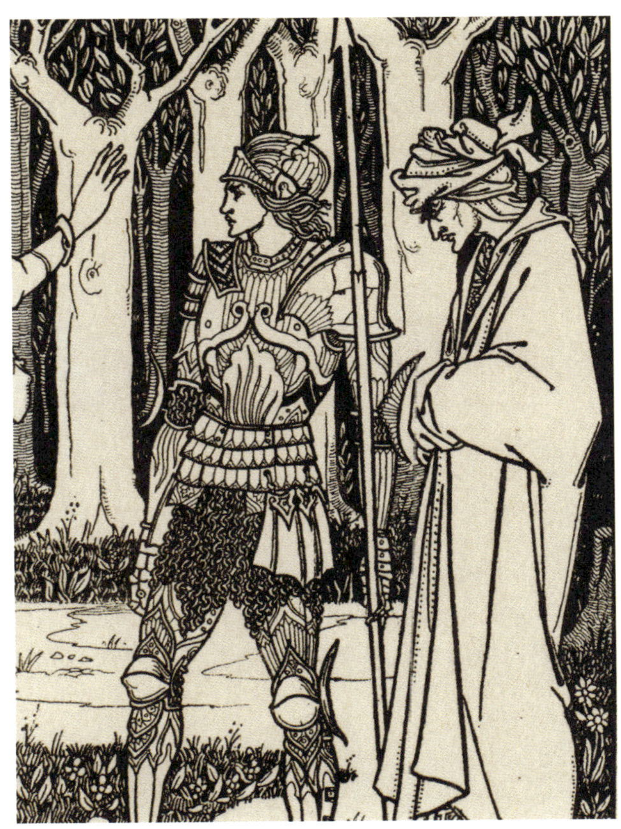

17. *The Lady of the Lake*, drawing for *Le Morte Darthur* by Thomas Malory, published by J.M. Dent & Co., London, 1893–4
Line block print
Victoria and Albert Museum, London
(V&A: E.406-1899)

In this scene the mysterious lady tells King Arthur of the magic sword Excalibur. The borders, composition, figures, forest and winding pathway follow the example set by Burne-Jones. Altogether for *Le Morte Darthur* Beardsley created 20 full- and double-page illustrations, 240 chapter headings, 43 borders, 25 initials, 19 ornaments and four ornamental headpieces – a total requiring a degree of invention that was excessive even for Beardsley.

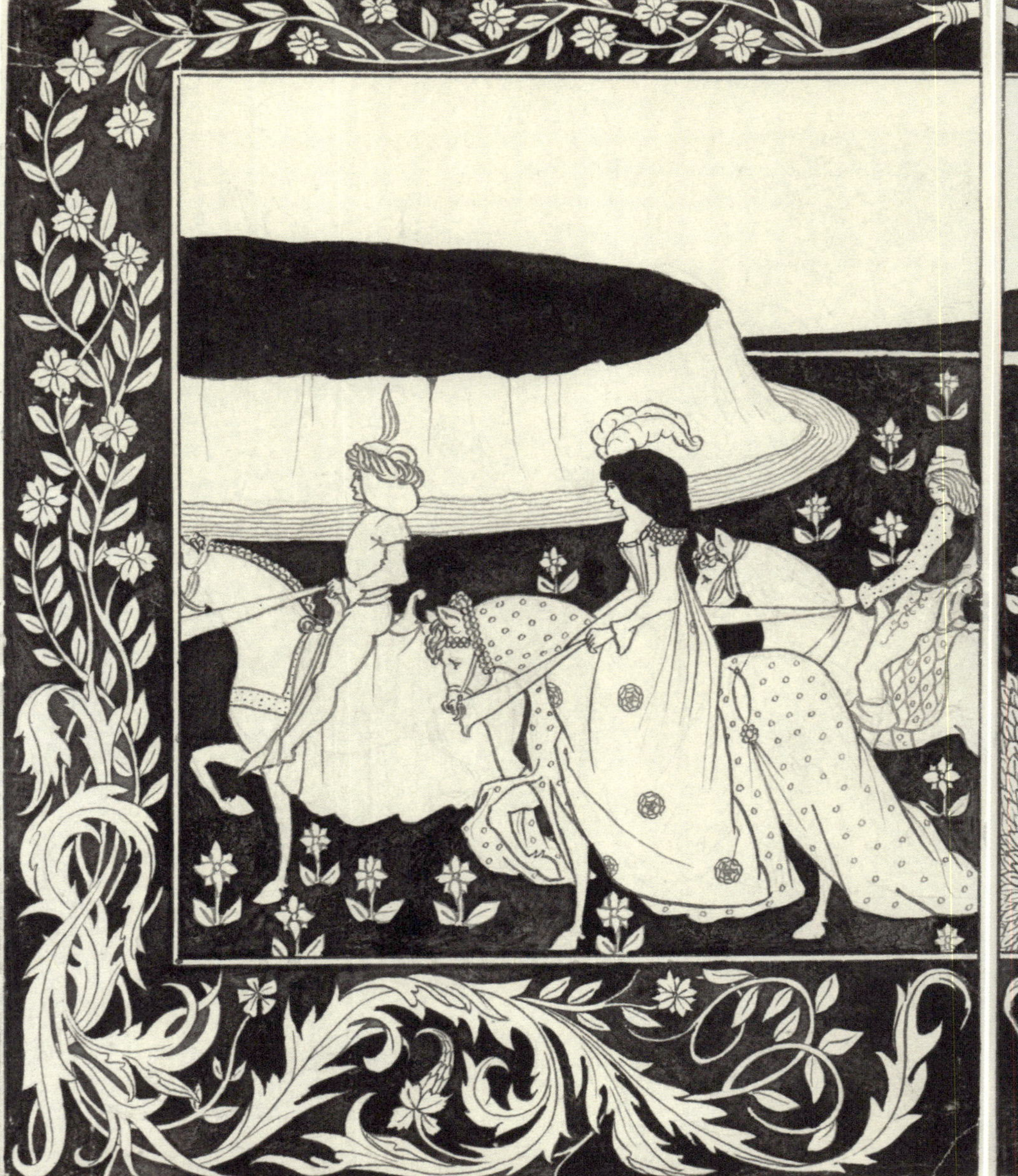

These two drawings for a double-page illustration depict this scene from *Le Morte Darthur*: 'SO it befell in the month of May, Queen Guenever called unto her knights of the Table Round; and she gave them warning that early upon the morrow she would ride a-Maying into woods and fields beside Westminster. And I warn you that there be none of you but that he be well horsed, and that ye all be clothed in green … and I shall bring with me ten ladies, and every knight shall have a lady behind him.'[55]

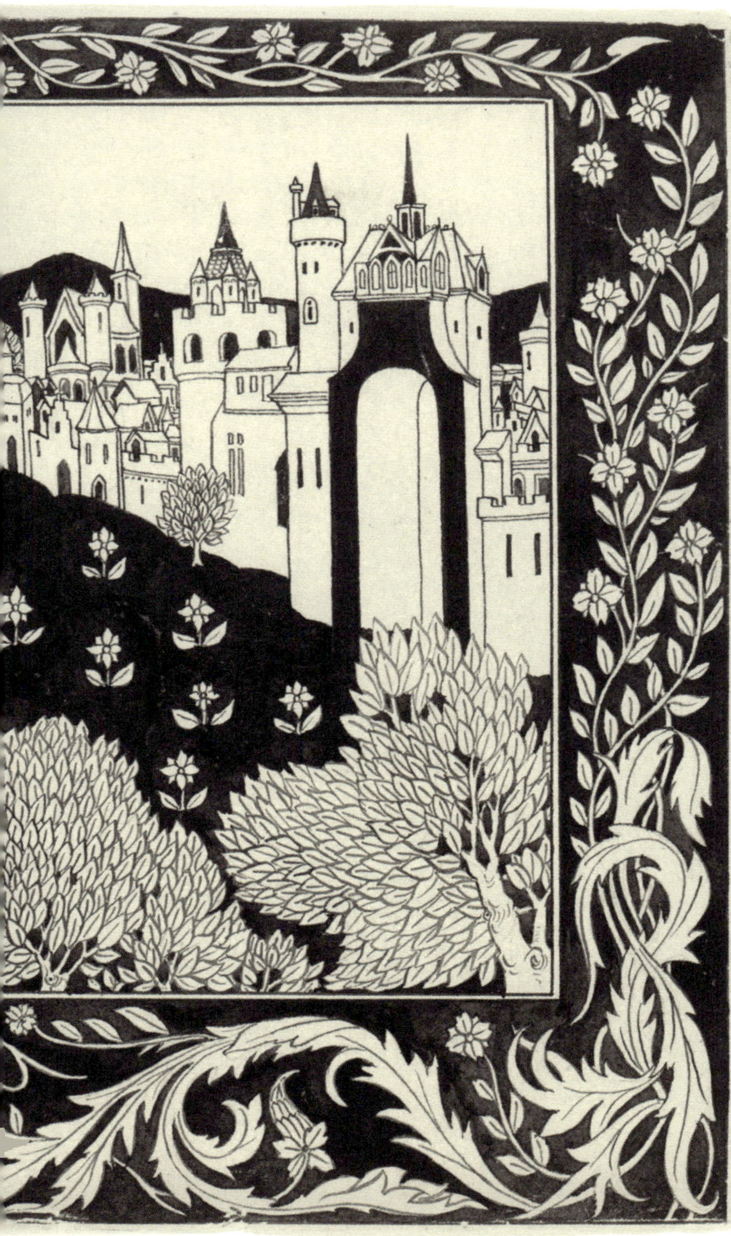

18. *How Queen Guenevere rode on Maying*, drawing for *Le Morte Darthur* by Thomas Malory, published by J.M. Dent & Co., London, 1893–4
Pen and Indian ink on paper
Victoria and Albert Museum, London
(V&A: E.290 and 291-1972)

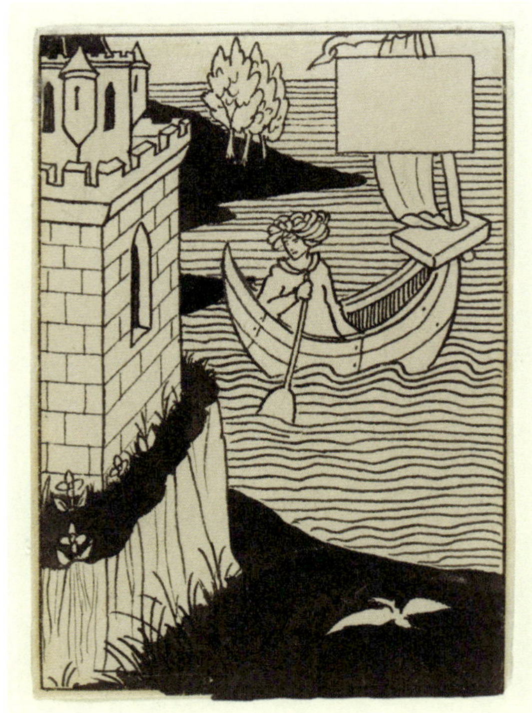

19. *How Sir Lancelot passed over the sea*, chapter heading for *Le Morte Darthur* by Thomas Malory, published by J.M. Dent & Co., London, 1893–4
Pen and ink on paper
Victoria and Albert Museum, London (V&A: E.423-1920)

'And so they shipped at Cardiff, and sailed unto Benwick: some men call it Bayonne, and some men call it Beaune, where the wine of Beaune is.'[56] This drawing illustrates an episode in *Le Morte Darthur* that relates Lancelot's voyage to France, where he ennobles his knightly companions in a list of names that Malory curtails, saying 'meseemeth it were too long to rehearse'. Here Beardsley imitates the archaic language with a deliberately naïve manner, skilfully echoing medieval woodcuts.

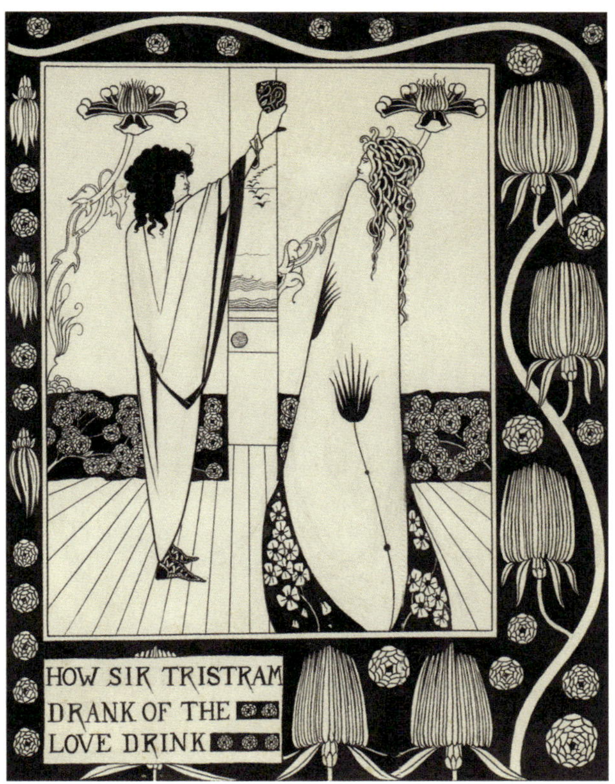

20. *How Sir Tristram Drank of the Love Drink*, drawing for *Le Morte Darthur* by Thomas Malory, published by J.M. Dent & Co., London, 1893–4
Graphite and ink on paper
Harvard Art Museums/Fogg Museum, Bequest of Scofield Thayer (1986.681)

The tragic affair between Sir Tristram and La Belle Isolde began on board ship when they shared an enchanted love potion. Beardsley's illustration shows triffid-like flowers encroaching diagonally on both figures, which are rendered with extreme stylization. Between them is a glimpse of the ocean, as on a stage set. This image anticipates Beardsley's later drawing of Salome and St John the Baptist (31).

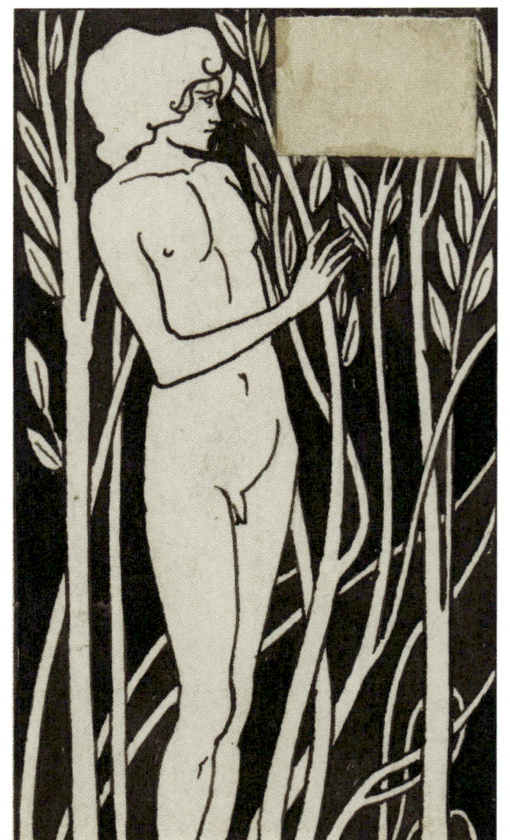

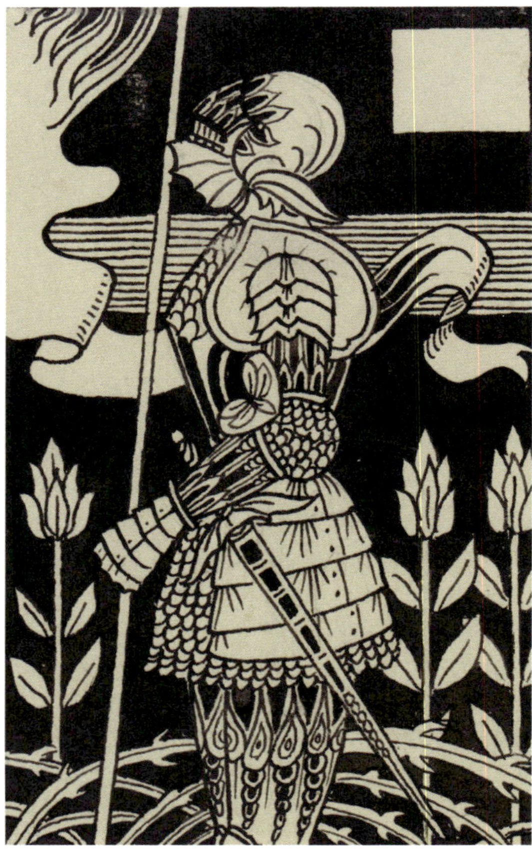

21. Chapter headings for *Le Morte Darthur* by Thomas Malory, published by J.M. Dent & Co., London, 1893–4
Pen and ink on paper
Victoria and Albert Museum, London (V&A: D.123-1899 and D.1827-1904)

The variety of Beardsley's images is well illustrated in his designs for *Le Morte Darthur*, which range from slender wood-sprites and summer maidens to the wizard Merlin and a fully armoured knight. Each meticulously drawn and inked ornament supports the late medieval setting of the Arthurian tales without creating yet more narratives to distract the reader.

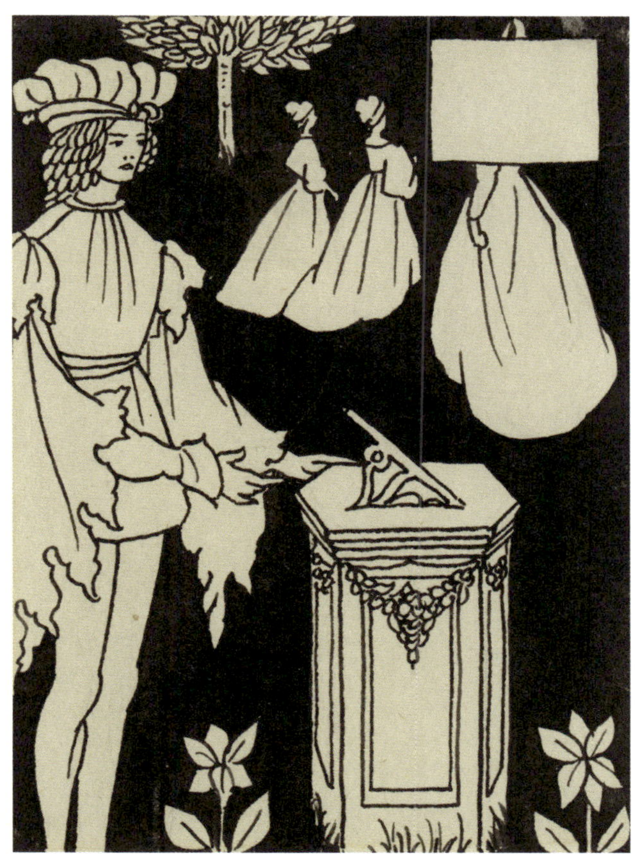

22. Chapter heading for *Le Morte Darthur* by Thomas Malory, published by J.M. Dent & Co., London, 1893–4
Pen and ink on paper
Victoria and Albert Museum, London
(V&A: D.1825-1904)

Before the *Morte Darthur* commission was complete, Beardsley had lost his enthusiasm for the project. He told Burne-Jones that '[h]e hated the story and he hated all medieval things'.[57] The careless drawing of the tree and flowers in this image suggests untypical weariness of spirit.

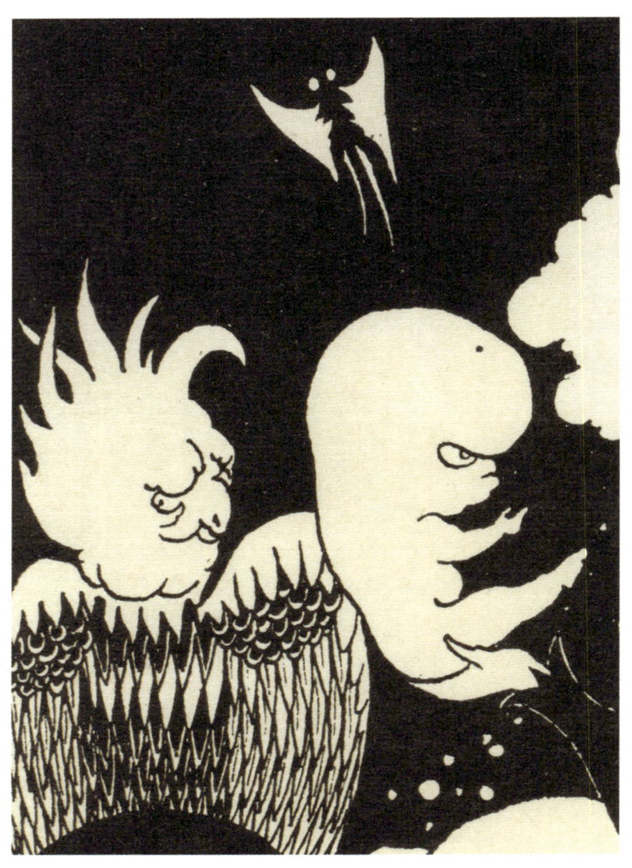

23. Illustration for *Vera Historia*, 1894
Line block print
Victoria and Albert Museum, London
(V&A: E.688-1945)

Beardsley's pictorial imagination was stimulated by a commission to illustrate *Vera Historia* (A True Story) by the classical author Lucian. This relates fantastic adventures with alien life-forms and alternate physical laws – notions conveyed in Beardsley's hybrid images, which are reminiscent of Hieronymus Bosch. Here a parrot, an embryo, a Valkyrie, a pierrot and a cobra are among the figures jostling for space.

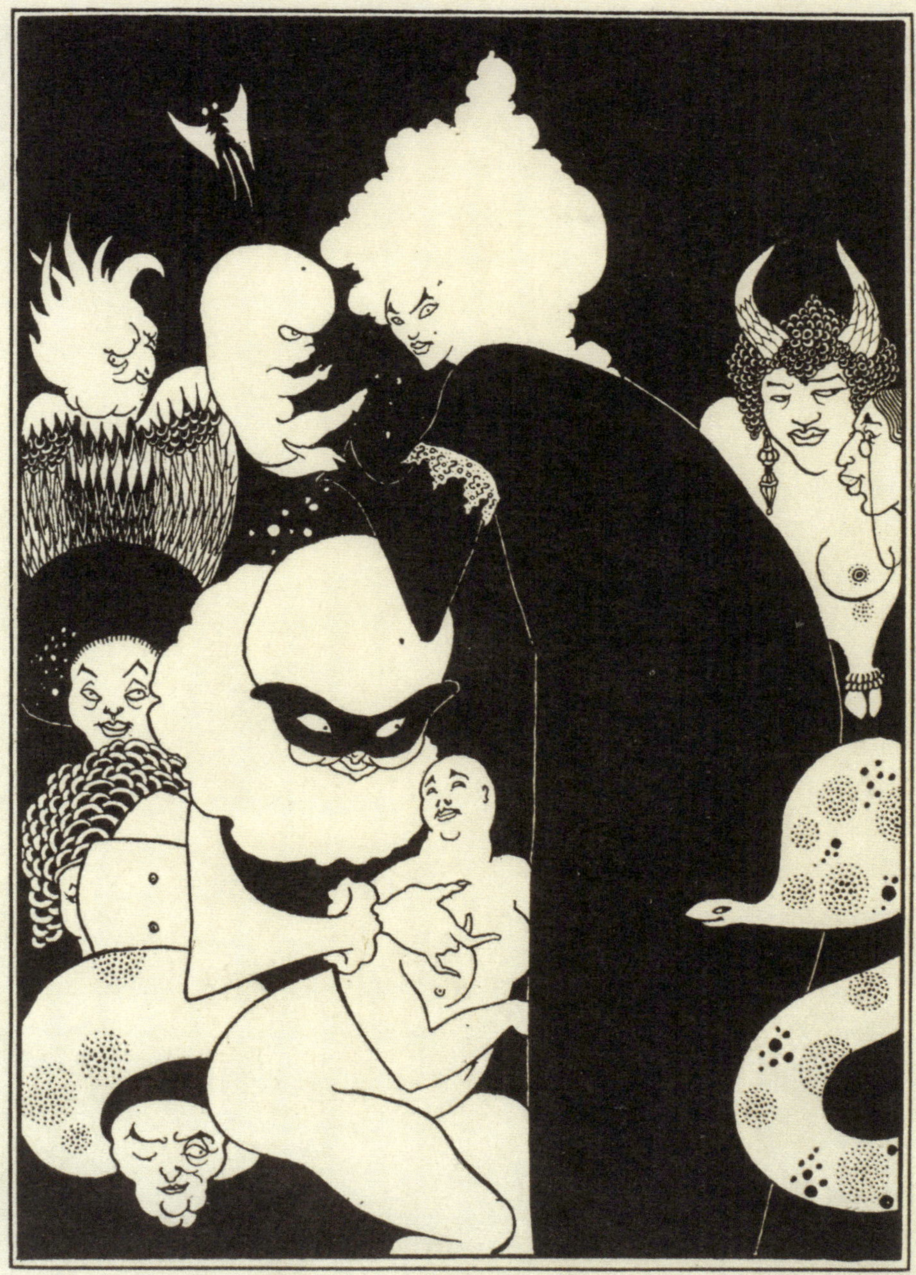

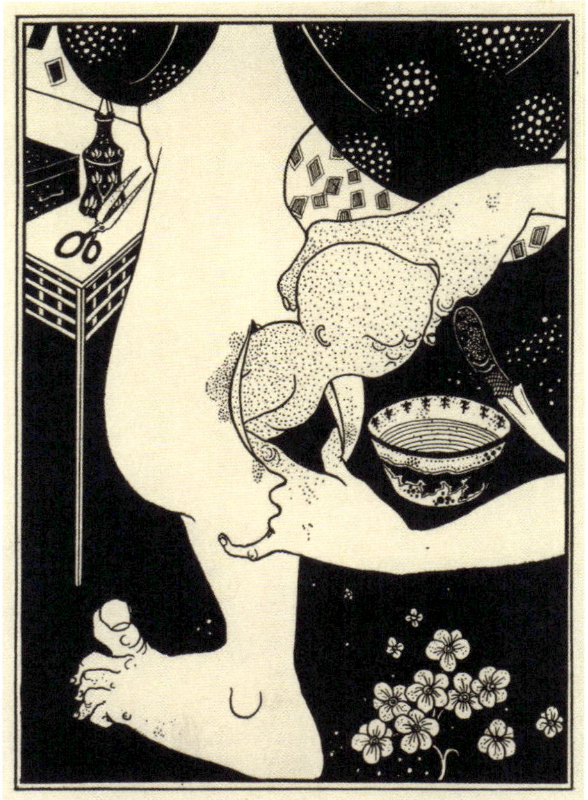

24. Illustration for *Vera Historia*, 1894
Line block print
Victoria and Albert Museum, London
(V&A: E.687-1945)

In an image that is both gruesome and comic, a foetus is cut from a human leg. Episodes in Lucian's *Vera Historia* invoke the 'monsters' that feature in ancient travellers' tales, and also prefigure the strange creatures encountered in science fantasy and space exploration movies. Both this and the previous design were in fact rejected as too grotesque for publication.

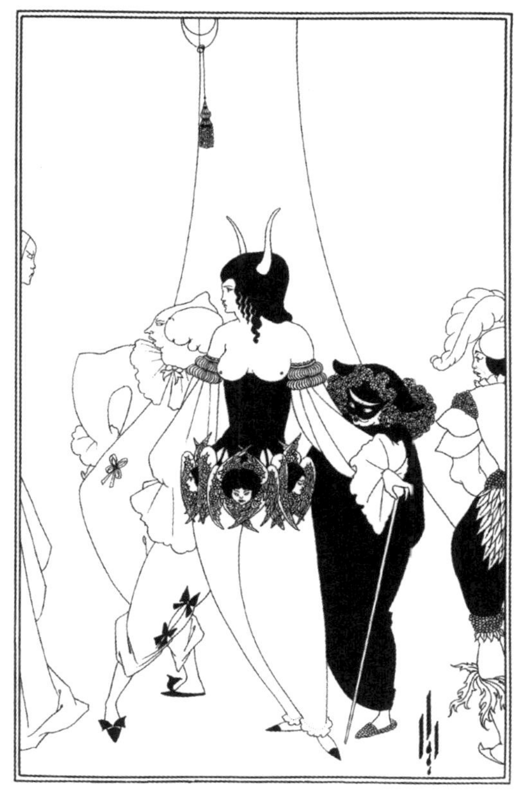

25. *The Masque of the Red Death*, 1894
Print
Private collection

The horror stories of Edgar Allan Poe led to a commission for Beardsley from a publisher in Chicago. In a short series that illustrated some uncanny scenes, the subjects gave free rein to Beardsley's taste for the macabre. The fee for each illustration was £5. Here a group of figures drawn from pantomime and nightmare represent the masquerade ball that Prince Prospero stages in a vain attempt to escape the Red Death, a mysterious plague.

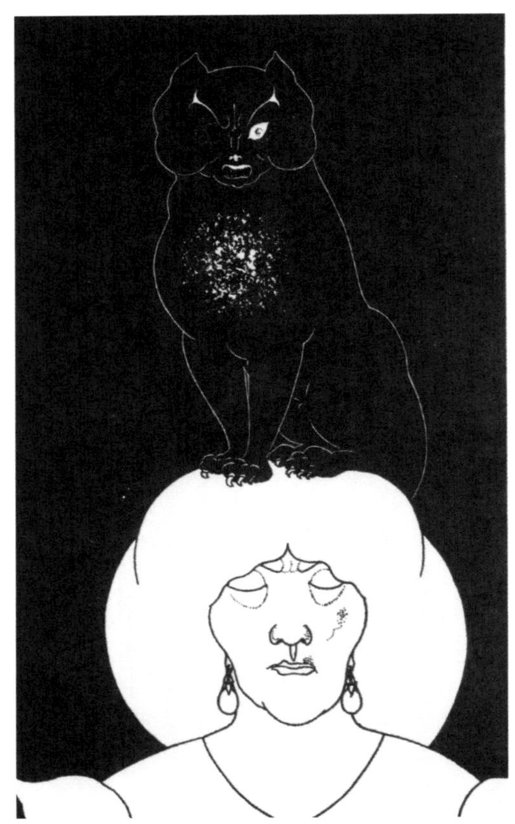

26. *The Black Cat*, 1894
Line block print
Library of Congress
(NC1115.B43)

A narrative of alcoholism and guilt, Poe's story *The Black Cat* tells of a man who gouges out one eye of the cat he loves and kills it, and is then haunted by its one-eyed double with a white patch. Later, in a drunken fury the man murders his wife, whose body he walls up with the cat, until it is discovered sitting on her decomposing head. The animal's malevolent stare, and the stark contrast of black and white, convey the story's inescapable horror.

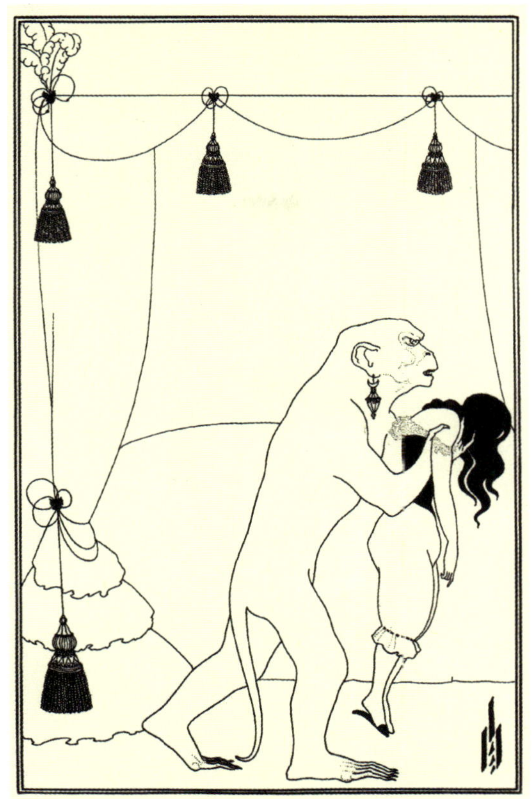

27. *The Murders in the rue Morgue*, 1894
Print
Library of Congress

Now regarded as the archetypal murder mystery, *The Murders in the rue Morgue* is Poe's best known story, frequently depicted in visual media. Here Beardsley presents a spoiler, revealing the killer as an orang-utan, which murders and mutilates a woman and her daughter in an apparently locked room. Victorian racial attitudes linking 'primitive' people with apes underlie Poe's plotline and Beardsley's picture.

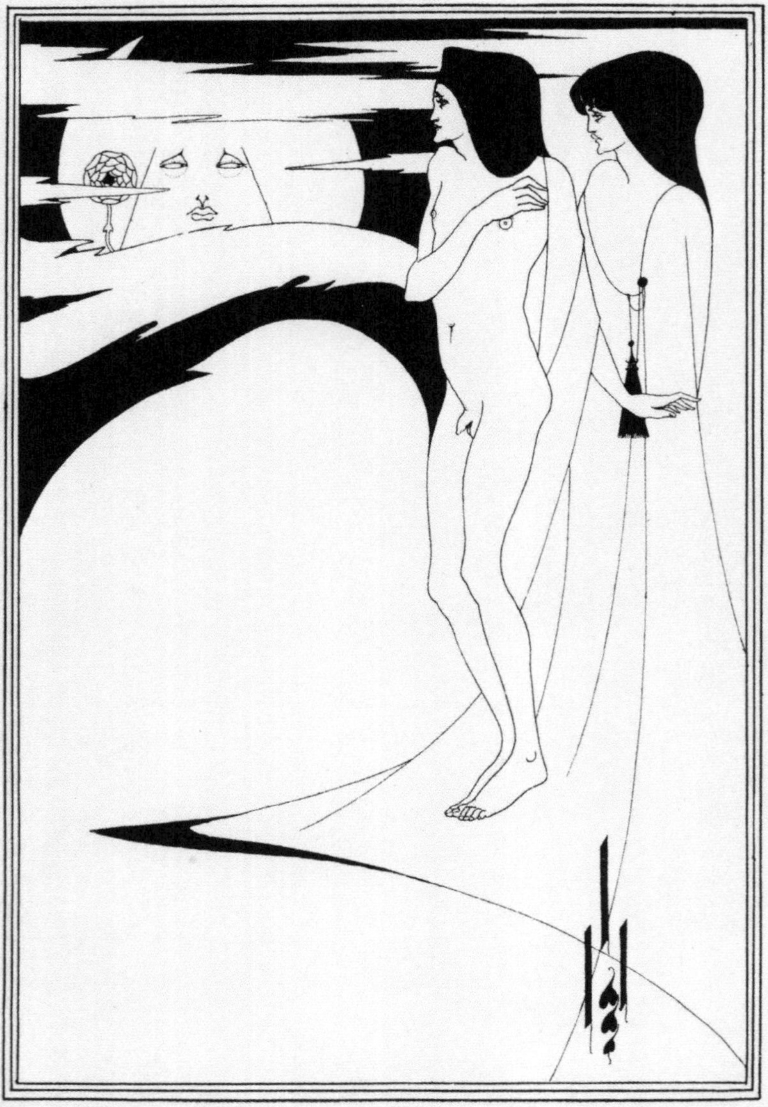

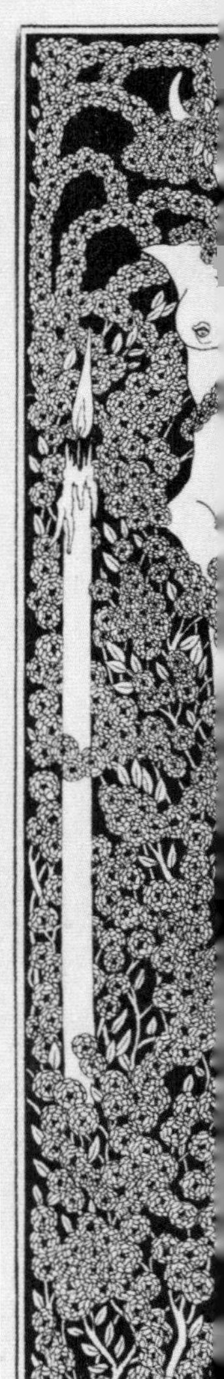

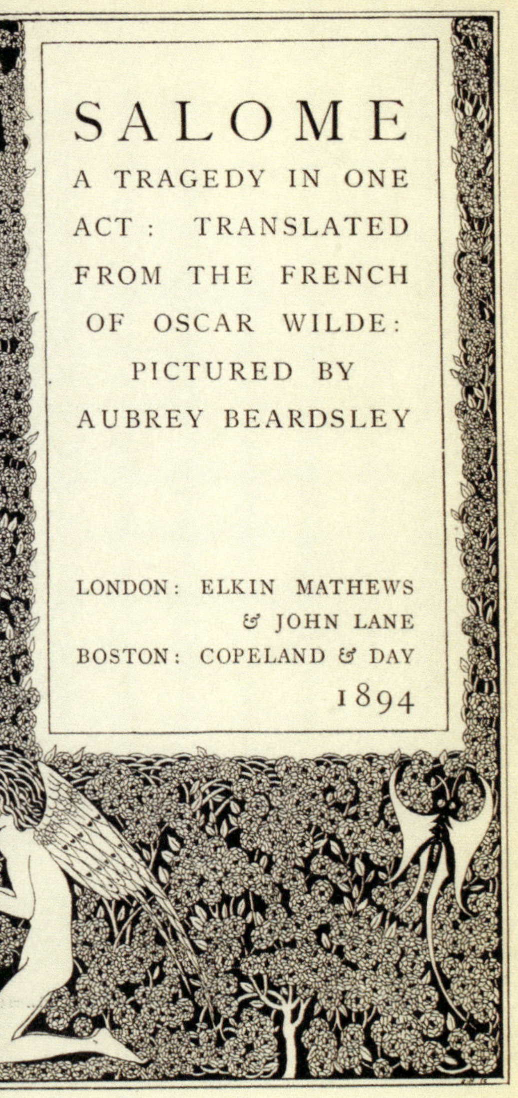

SALOME
A TRAGEDY IN ONE ACT: TRANSLATED FROM THE FRENCH OF OSCAR WILDE: PICTURED BY AUBREY BEARDSLEY

LONDON: ELKIN MATHEWS & JOHN LANE
BOSTON: COPELAND & DAY
1894

Beardsley's illustrated edition of Oscar Wilde's verse drama *Salome* is a masterpiece of sinister and interpretive imagery, ranging freely within and beyond the text. In the frontispiece a young couple gaze towards a rising moon, which has Wilde's features. The clean arabesques of the image contrast with the teeming blossoms of the title page opposite. On the original design both the kneeling Eros (Cupid) and the androgynous herm (on the pillar) have male genitals.

28. *The Woman in the Moon* (plate I) and title page from *A Portfolio of Aubrey Beardsley's drawings illustrating 'Salome' by Oscar Wilde*, published by John Lane, London, 1907 (first published 1894)
Line block print on Japanese vellum
Victoria and Albert Museum, London
(V&A: C.22146:1)

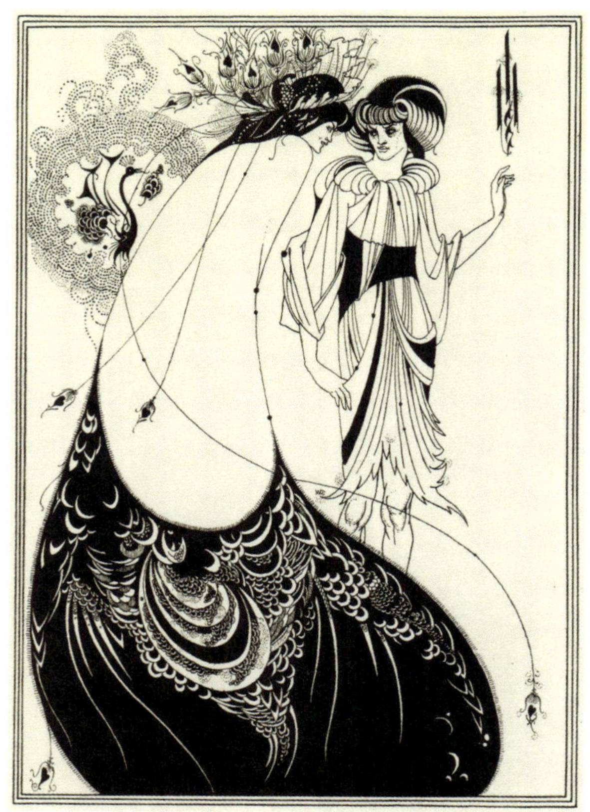

29. *The Peacock Skirt,* plate V from *A Portfolio of Aubrey Beardsley's drawings illustrating 'Salome' by Oscar Wilde,* published by John Lane, London, 1907 (first published 1894)
Line block print on Japanese vellum
Victoria and Albert Museum, London (V&A: E.426-1972)
Given by Michael Harari, in memory of his father, Ralph A. Harari

'How beautiful is the Princess Salomé to-night!' declares the young Syrian captain in the first scene of the play. 'She is like a narcissus trembling in the wind … She is like a silver flower.' With commanding lines and alluring details, Beardsley's image of Salome and the captain pays homage to the peacock motifs favoured by J.A.M. Whistler, to dramatic contemporary fashions and to the emerging notion of the sexually dominant New Woman.

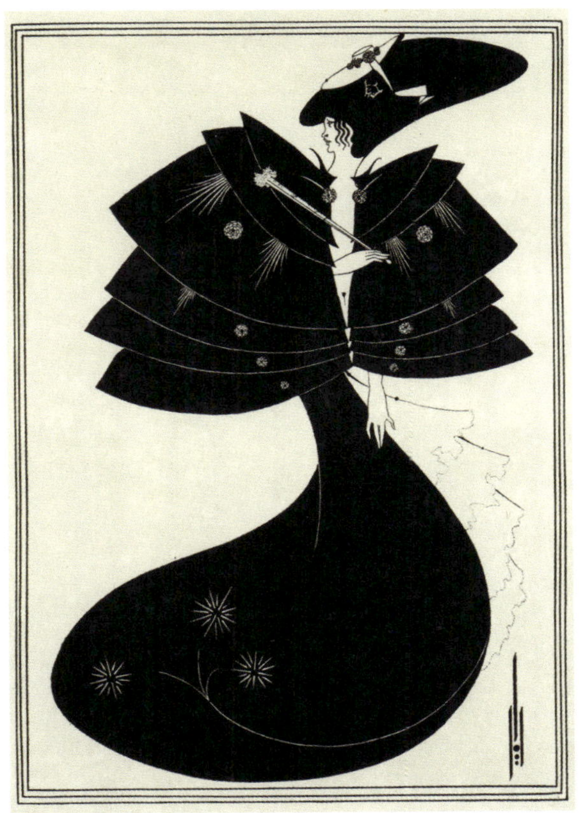

30. *The Black Cape*, plate VI from *A Portfolio of Aubrey Beardsley's drawings illustrating 'Salome' by Oscar Wilde*, published by John Lane, London, 1907 (first published 1894)
Line block print on Japanese vellum
Victoria and Albert Museum, London (V&A: E.427-1972)
Given by Michael Harari, in memory of his father, Ralph A. Harari

Here Beardsley depicts a woman wearing a wildly exaggerated version of women's fashions in the 1890s, with layered and ruched shoulders, long, high-waisted skirts and large elaborate hats. 'The Princess rises! She is leaving the table!' exclaims the Syrian at this point in the play. 'She looks very troubled. Ah, she is coming this way. Yes, she is coming towards us. How pale she is! Never have I seen her so pale.'

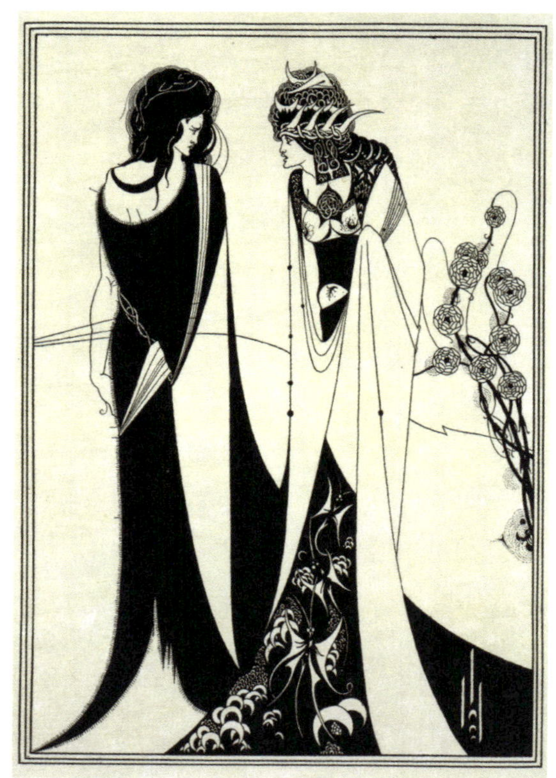

31. *John and Salome*, plate VIII from *A Portfolio of Aubrey Beardsley's drawings illustrating 'Salome' by Oscar Wilde*, published by John Lane, London, 1907 (first published 1894)
Line block print on Japanese vellum
Victoria and Albert Museum, London (V&A: E.429-1972)
Given by Michael Harari, in memory of his father, Ralph A. Harari

Two figures held in mesmeric mutual gaze is one of Beardsley's favoured motifs; here the elongated figures of John the Baptist (called Jokanaan in the drama) and Salome rise like coupled snakes, with malevolent feeling. 'It is thy mouth that I desire, Jokanaan', says Salome, as Beardsley's curving shapes echo Wilde's lines. 'It is like a pomegranate cut with a knife of ivory. The pomegranate-flowers that blossom in the gardens of Tyre, and are redder than roses, are not so red.'

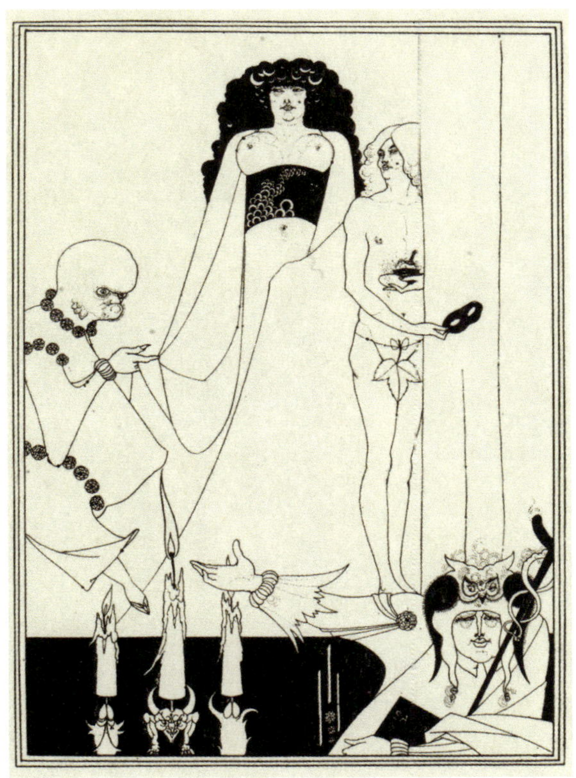

32. *Enter Herodias*, plate IX from *A Portfolio of Aubrey Beardsley's drawings illustrating 'Salome' by Oscar Wilde*, published by John Lane, London, 1907 (first published 1894)
Line block print on Japanese vellum
Victoria and Albert Museum, London
(V&A: E.412-1899)

'Art thou not afraid, daughter of Herodias?' asks Jokanaan as Salome's mother, Herodias, enters the scene. 'Did I not tell thee that I had heard in the palace the beatings of the wings of the angel of death?' Here Herodias is flanked by phallic candles and deformed creatures, the one at bottom right caricaturing Oscar Wilde. The drawings were 'as stupid as they could be', said Burne-Jones. 'Empty of any great quality and detestable.'[58]

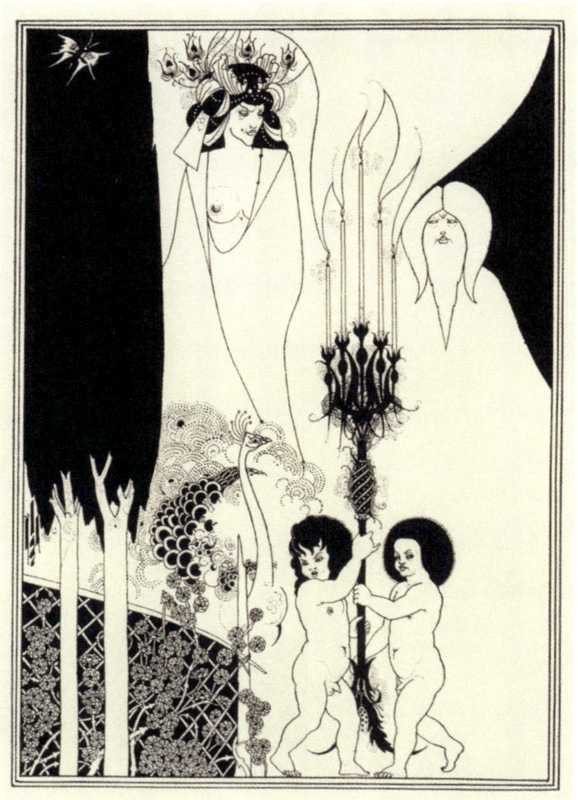

33. *The Eyes of Herod*, plate X from *A Portfolio of Aubrey Beardsley's drawings illustrating 'Salome' by Oscar Wilde*, published by John Lane, London, 1907 (first published 1894)
Line block print on Japanese vellum
Victoria and Albert Museum, London (V&A: E.431-1972)
Given by Michael Harari, in memory of his father, Ralph A. Harari

This is the most fanciful of the Salome illustrations, in which forms are ambiguously delineated, mimicking the disjointed dramatic dialogue. Salome (top centre) floats between cypress trees and flames, and Beardsley also includes a peacock, two putti and a bearded moon-like head. 'The moon has a strange look to-night,' says Herod at this point in the text. 'She reels through the clouds like a drunken woman … I am sure she is looking for lovers.'

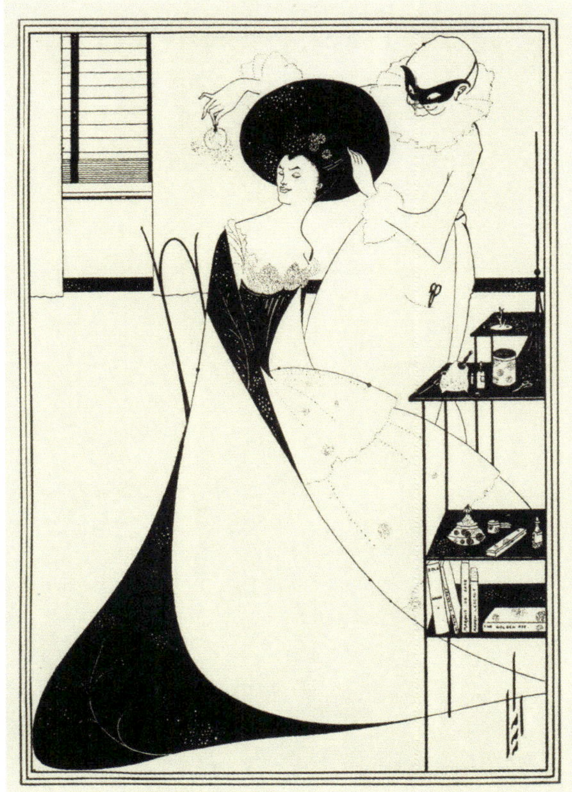

34. *The Toilette of Salome II*, plate XII from *A Portfolio of Aubrey Beardsley's drawings illustrating 'Salome' by Oscar Wilde*, published by John Lane, London, 1907 (first published 1894)
Line block print on Japanese vellum
Victoria and Albert Museum, London (V&A: E.433-1972)
Given by Michael Harari, in memory of his father, Ralph A. Harari

Only a few blocks of black prevent this from being an outline drawing; extravagant swoops are anchored in strong horizontal and vertical framing. Tended by a coiffeur in pierrot costume, Salome becomes an almost disembodied art nouveau poster girl, albeit with a menacing air. 'A huge black bird … hovers over the terrace,' declares Herod at this point in the play. 'The beat of its wings is terrible.'

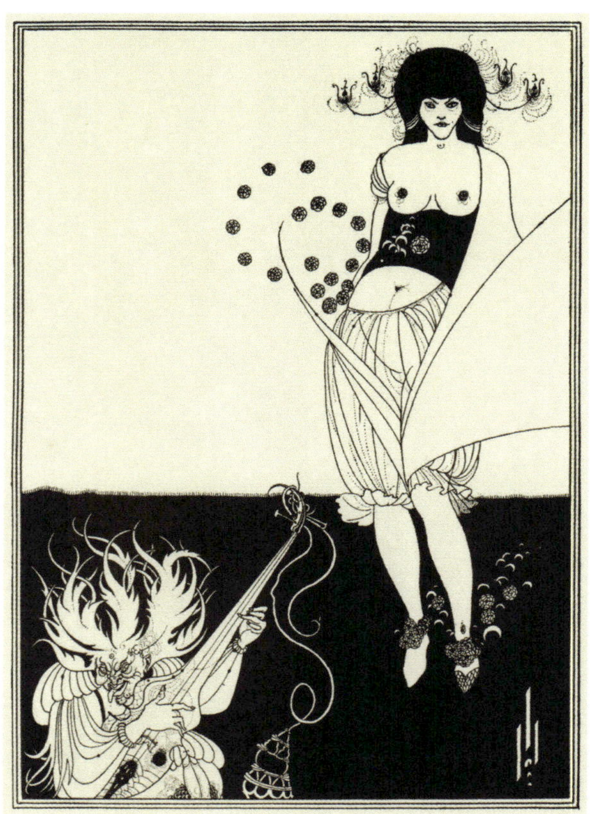

35. *The Stomach Dance*, plate XI from *A Portfolio of Aubrey Beardsley's drawings illustrating 'Salome' by Oscar Wilde*, published by John Lane, London, 1907 (first published 1894)
Line block print on Japanese vellum
Victoria and Albert Museum, London (V&A: E.432-1972)
Given by Michael Harari, in memory of his father, Ralph A. Harari

'Ah! the wanton! The harlot! Ah! the daughter of Babylon with her golden eyes and her gilded eyelids!' declaims Jokanaan, 'Let the people take stones and stone her.' As Salome performs her dance of the Seven Veils, portrayed as if on a music-hall stage, with a demonic musician, Jokanaan's denunciation could be aimed at the godless contemporary audience.

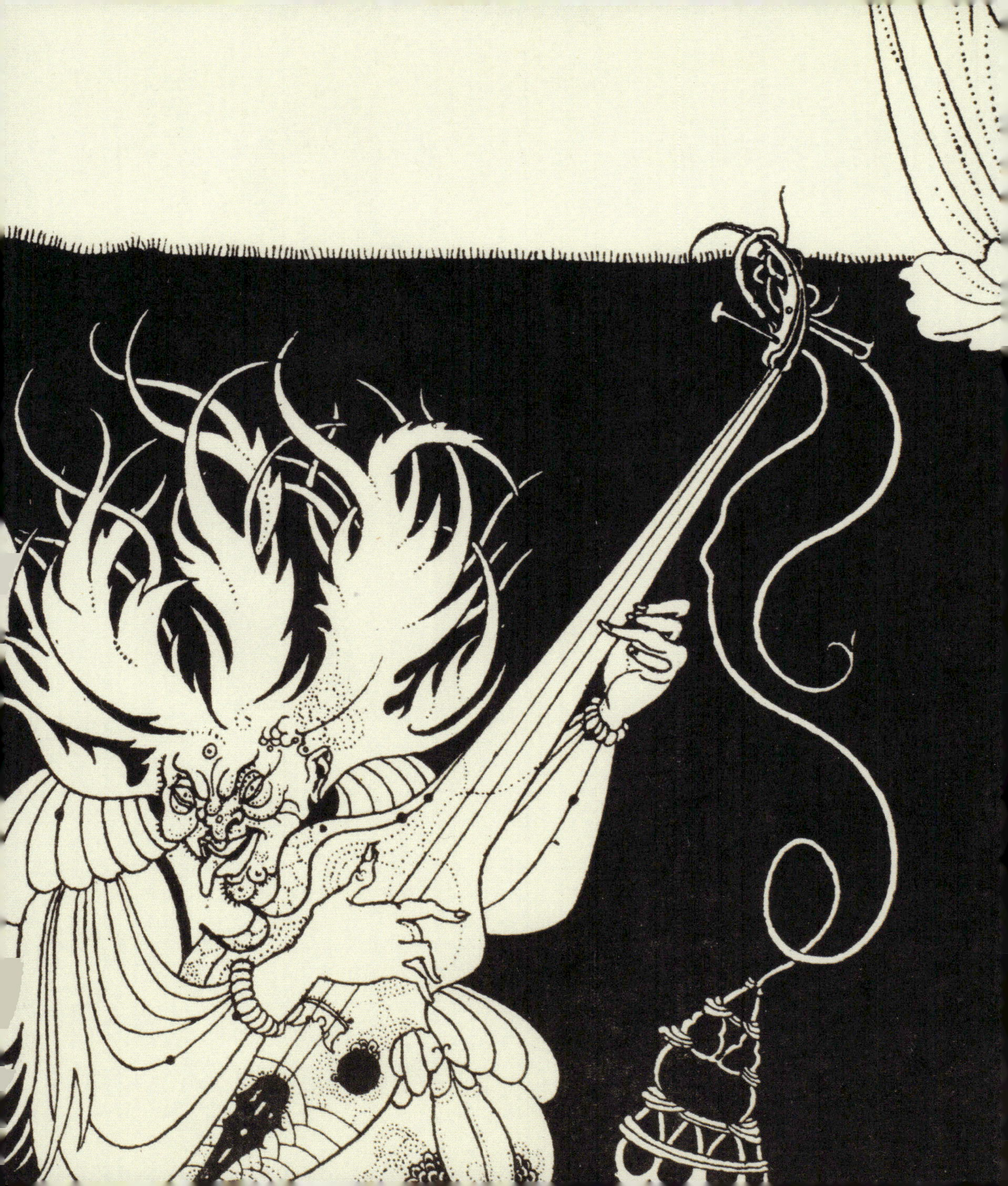

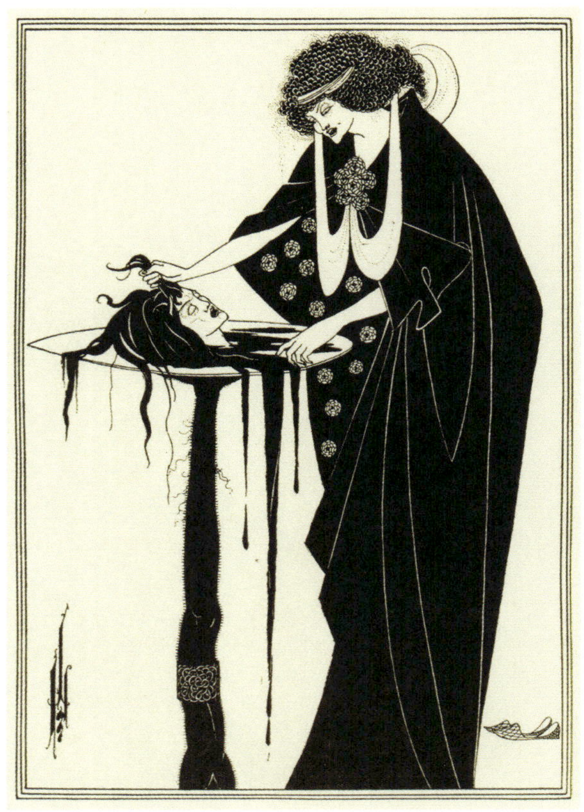

36. *The Dancer's Reward*, plate XIV from *A Portfolio of Aubrey Beardsley's drawings illustrating 'Salome' by Oscar Wilde*, published by John Lane, London, 1907 (first published 1894)
Line block print on Japanese vellum
Victoria and Albert Museum, London (V&A: E.435-1972)
Given by Michael Harari, in memory of his father, Ralph A. Harari

A huge black arm, the arm of the Executioner, comes forth from the cistern, bearing on a silver shield the head of Jokanaan. Salome seizes it. 'It is for mine own pleasure that I ask the head of Jokanaan in a silver charger', says Salome. 'You hath sworn, Herod. Forget not that you have sworn an oath. … Command your soldiers that they bring me the head of Jokanaan.'

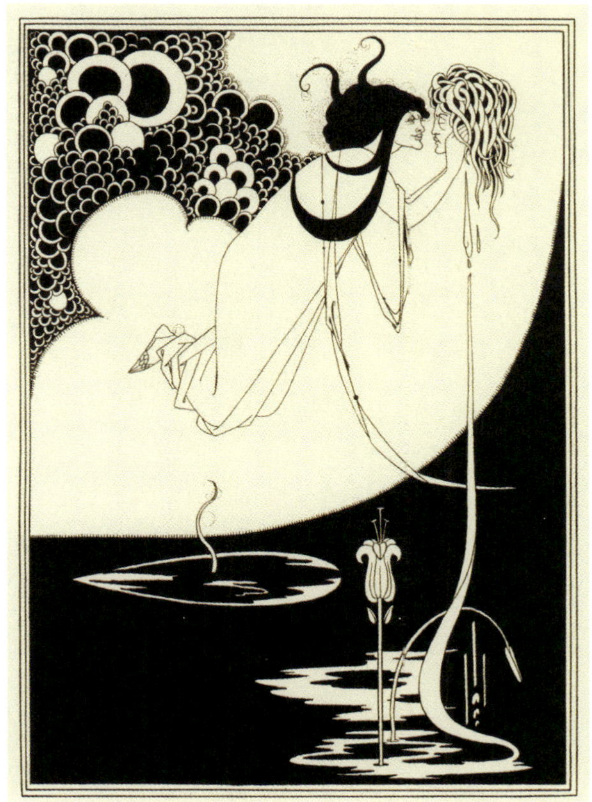

37. *The Climax*, plate XV from *A Portfolio of Aubrey Beardsley's drawings illustrating 'Salome' by Oscar Wilde*, published by John Lane, London, 1907 (first published 1894)
Line block print on Japanese vellum
Victoria and Albert Museum, London (V&A: E.436-1972)
Given by Michael Harari, in memory of his father, Ralph A. Harari

'Thou wouldst not suffer me to kiss thy mouth, Jokanaan. Well! I will kiss it now. I will bite it with my teeth as one bites a ripe fruit. Yes, I will kiss thy mouth, Jokanaan. I said it; did I not say it?' This most notorious and most Decadent illustration offers a vividly surreal vision of Salome holding Jokanaan's severed head, as darkness falls on the drama. 'Put out the torches! Hide the moon! Hide the stars!' orders Herod. 'I begin to be afraid. Kill that woman!'

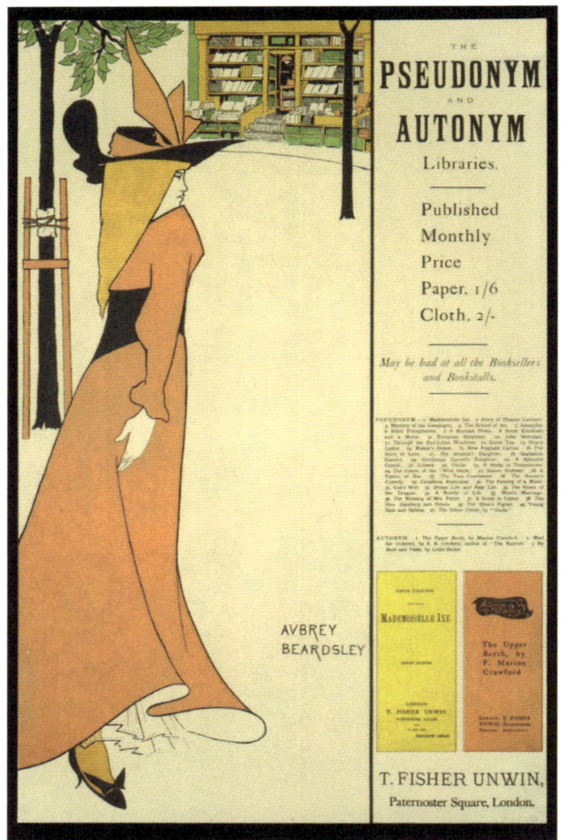

38. *This Pseudonym and Autonym Libraries*, poster advertising a series of books published by T. Fisher Unwin, 1894
Colour lithograph
Victoria and Albert Museum, London (V&A: E.1376-1931)

Beardsley's distinctive style brought commercial commissions for reproduction using the latest colour lithographic printing, often in off-beat hues. Posters and placards were perfectly shaped for his stylish, elongated female figures. Here two main themes, a fashionable woman and a bookstore, are combined in a publisher's advertisement. In the 1890s avant-garde fiction and verse became identified with this graphic style.

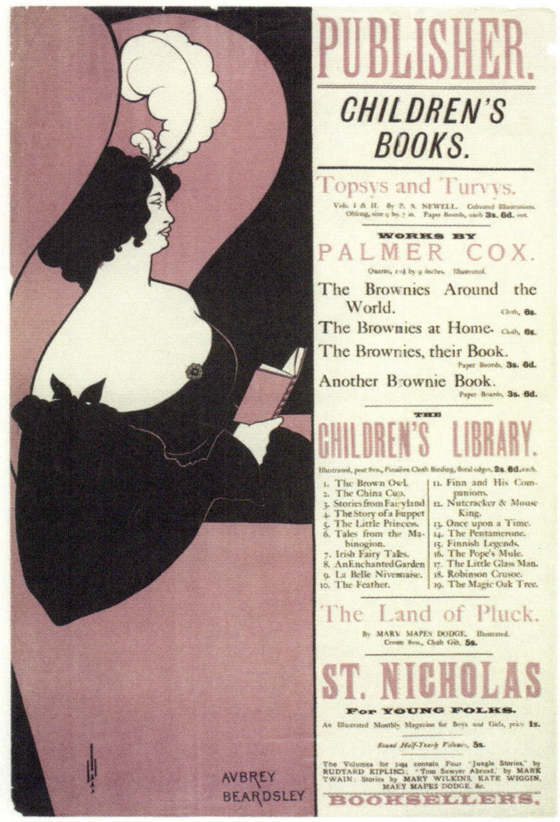

39. *Publisher. Children's Books*, poster advertising children's books published by T. Fisher Unwin, 1894
Colour lithograph
Victoria and Albert Museum, London
(V&A: E.956-1966)

While this sophisticated woman, wearing a low-cut gown and the ostrich-feather ornament popularized by Lillie Langtry (lover of the Prince of Wales), could be reading stories about brownies to her children, her bold, graphic demeanour seems quite unsuitable for 'young folks'. The lithographic printing process allows for other colourways, but mauve is a typically Decadent hue.

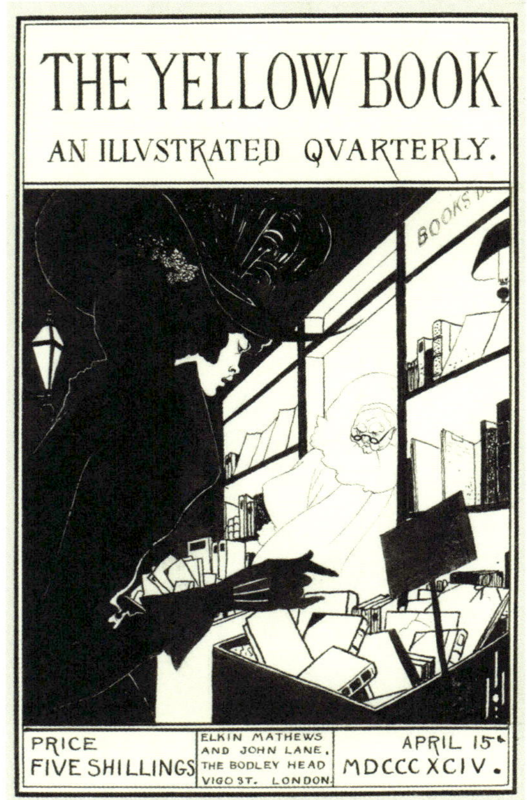

40. Design for the prospectus of *The Yellow Book*, vol. I, 1894, published by Elkin Mathews and John Lane of The Bodley Head, London, 1894
Pen and Indian ink on paper
Victoria and Albert Museum, London (V&A: E.518-1926)
Bequeathed by John Lane, Esq.

The Yellow Book promoted the New Woman in this cover design, demonstrating her independence to browse unchaperoned outside a bookstore in the evening. The transgressive nature of this activity is encoded in the white light from the shop window, thrown onto the dark shapes of the woman's figure. The face of the bookseller in the doorway, costumed as a clown, was drawn from Elkin Mathews, the co-publisher.

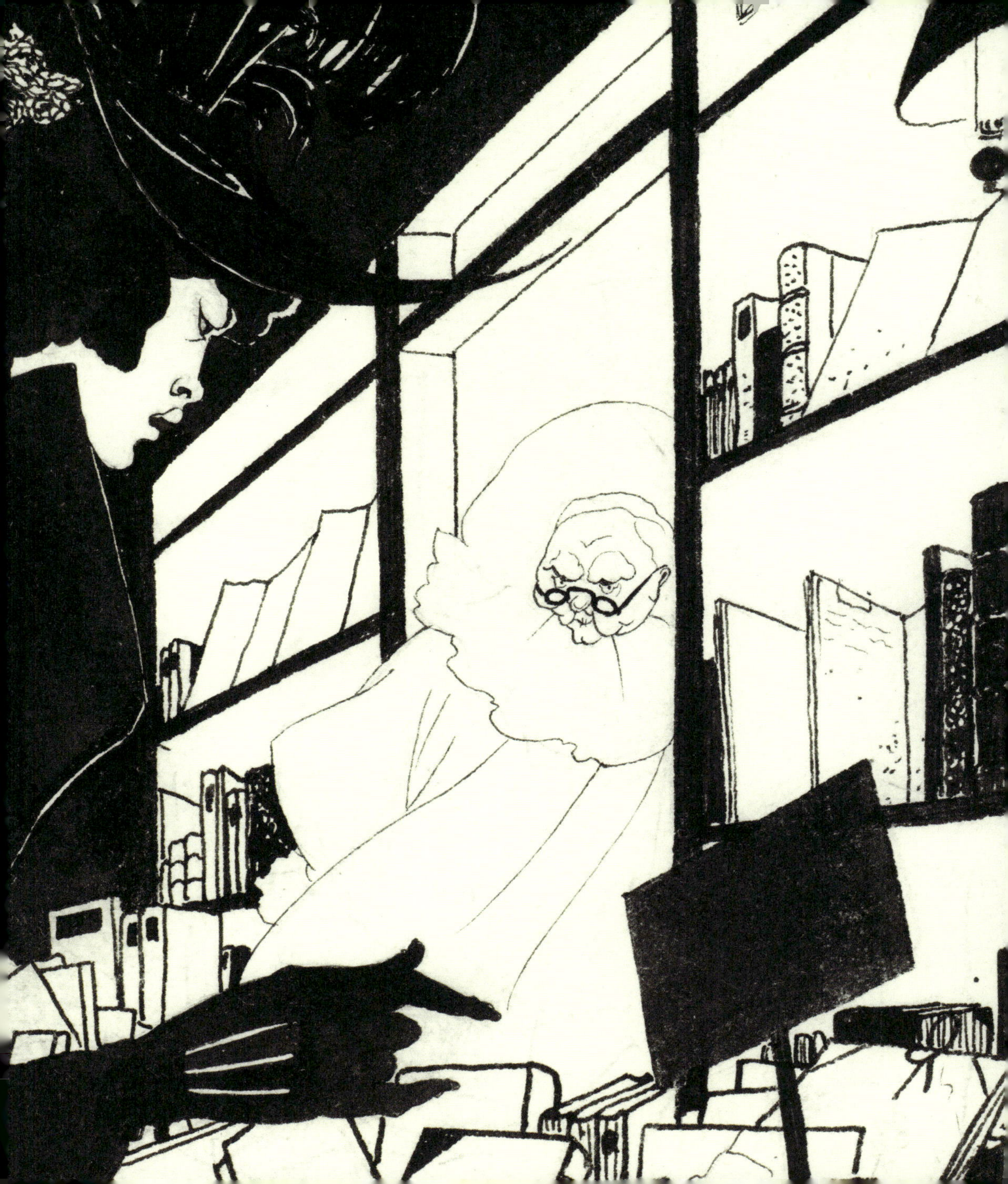

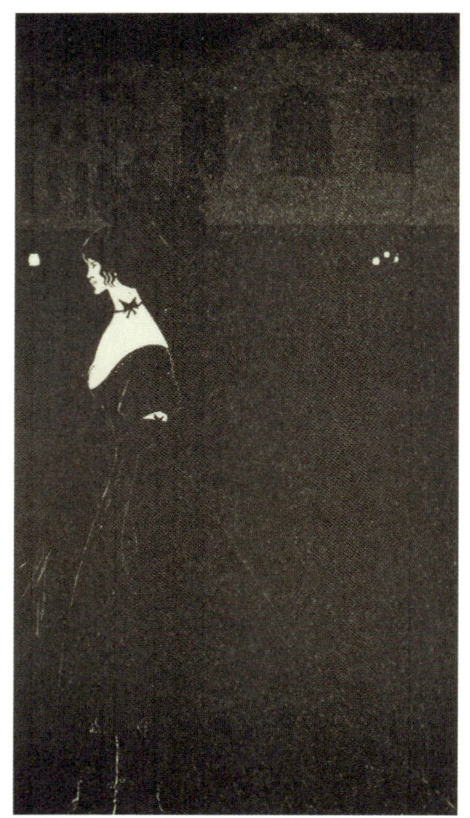

41. *A Night Piece*,
for *The Yellow Book*, 1894
Line block and gravure print
Victoria and Albert Museum, London
(V&A: E.1091-1996)

'I filled the window of the little shop with *Yellow Books*, and nothing but *Yellow Books*,' wrote a sales assistant recalling the launch of the first issue, 'creating such a mighty glow of yellow at the far end of Vigo Street that one might have been forgiven for imagining that some awful portent had happened, and that the sun had risen in the West.'[59] Beardsley's image depicts a streetwalker in London's Leicester Square.

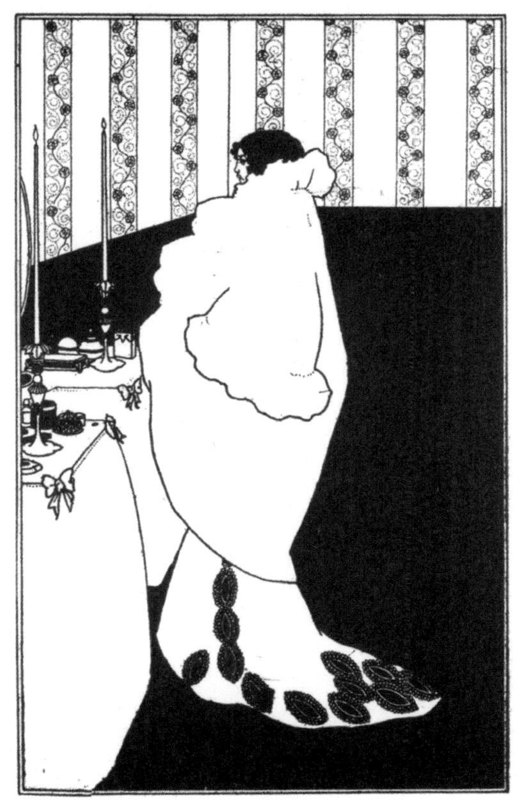

42. *La Dame aux Camélias*, for *The Yellow Book*, 1894
Line block print
Victoria and Albert Museum, London
(V&A: E.1088-1996)

The novel, opera, play and ballet *La Dame aux Camélias* tell the tragic tale, famously acted by Sarah Bernhardt from the 1880s onwards, of a courtesan who chooses red or white camellias to indicate her menstrual state – exactly the type of forbidden topic to appeal to *Yellow Book* readers. 'There seems to be a peculiar tendency in Mr. Beardsley's mind to the representation of types without intellect and without morals,' wrote one contemporary.[60]

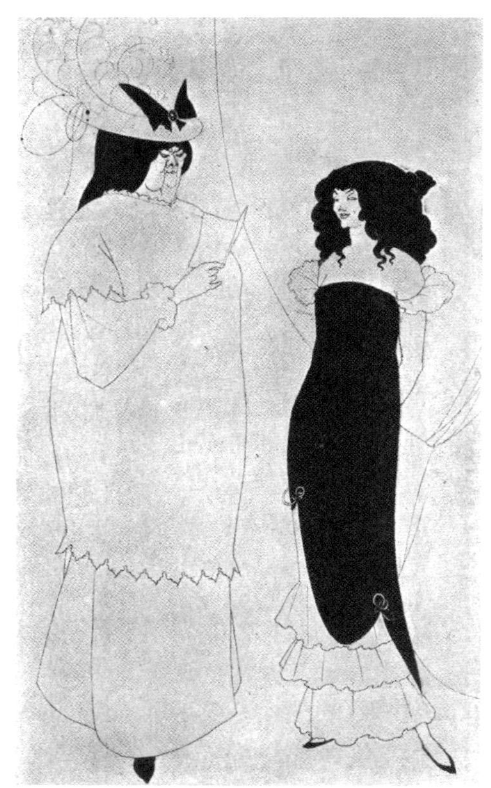

43. *L'Education Sentimentale*, for *The Yellow Book*, 1895
Line block and halftone print
Victoria and Albert Museum, London (V&A: E.1093-1996)

'Beardsley is a Decadent, and must do as the Decadents do,' wrote a contemporary critic; 'he must gloat upon ugliness and add to it; and when it is not there, he must create it.'[61] This drawing, its title borrowed from Gustave Flaubert's 1869 novel about a young man's passion for an older woman, satirizes a 'fat elderly whore'[62] instructing a slim girl – or perhaps is using the device of a theatrical curtain to imply the inevitable transformation of the latter into the former.

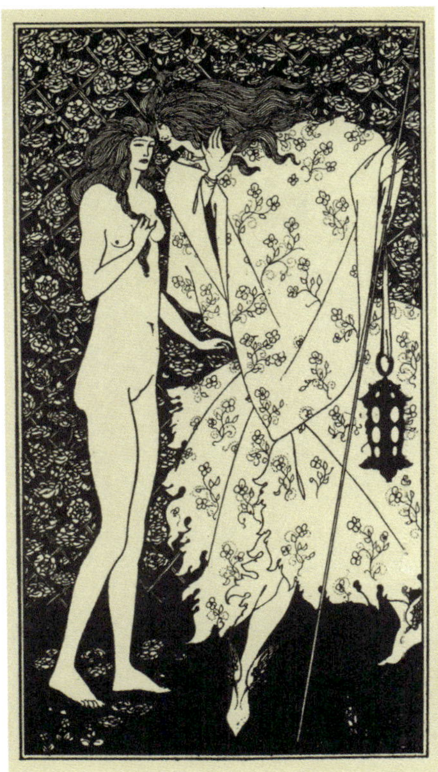

44. *The Mysterious Rose Garden*, for *The Yellow Book*, 1895
Pen and Indian ink on paper
Victoria and Albert Museum, London (V&A: E.379-1899)

This overly patterned image contains diverse allusions – to Eve in the Garden, to the Angel of the Annunciation (the figure with flames on his heels), and (via the lantern) to William Holman Hunt's painting *The Light of the World* (1851–3). For one historian, Beardsley's representation of the Virgin Mary's appointment with divine grace becomes a rose-trellis tryst with a Restoration rake,[63] who surely also has a cat's face. Whatever their identity, the couple's close encounter has dynamic force.

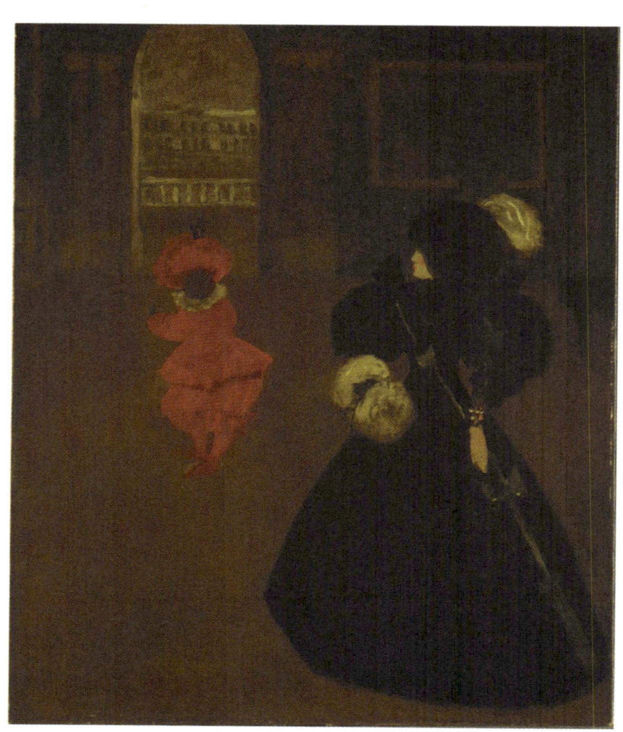

45. *A Caprice*, *c.*1894
Oil on canvas
Tate
(N03815 recto)

One of two oil pictures painted by Beardsley on both sides of one canvas, this painting relates to a trio of *Yellow Book* designs entitled *The Comedy Ballet of Marionettes.* In pictorial homage to Diego Velázquez (1599–1660), whose works were shown in London in spring 1893 and who painted the Madrid court dwarf and jester Sebastián de Morra, the red-clad dwarf in Spanish costume invites the woman through a doorway.

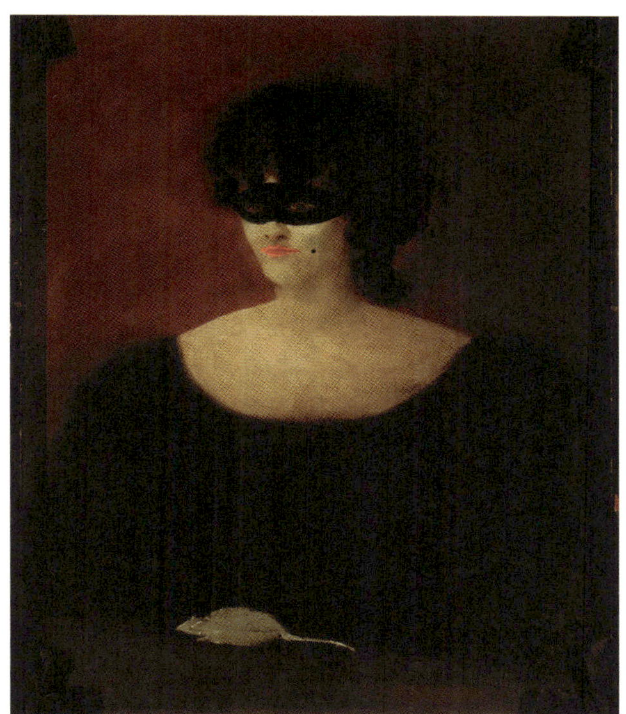

46. *Masked woman with white mouse*, *c*.1894
Oil on canvas
Tate
(N03815 verso)

Overleaf Vignette from *Bon-Mots of Samuel Foote and Theodore Hook*, edited by Walter Jerrold and published by J.M. Dent & Co., London, 1894, p. 101
Pen and ink on paper
Victoria and Albert Museum, London
(V&A: E.330-1972)

This unsettling image of a woman, seated on a balcony or box at the theatre, with a quasi-surreal mouse or rat, is painted on the back of *A Caprice* (45). The tonal qualities echo the dark, enigmatic images of Walter Sickert, a contributor to *The Yellow Book*, who also painted Beardsley's portrait. Highly sexualized interpretations have been offered for both this and *A Caprice*, but the works are 'unfinished, and should be regarded as experimental'.[64]

‘No one more than myself welcomes frank, nay hostile criticism’

1895

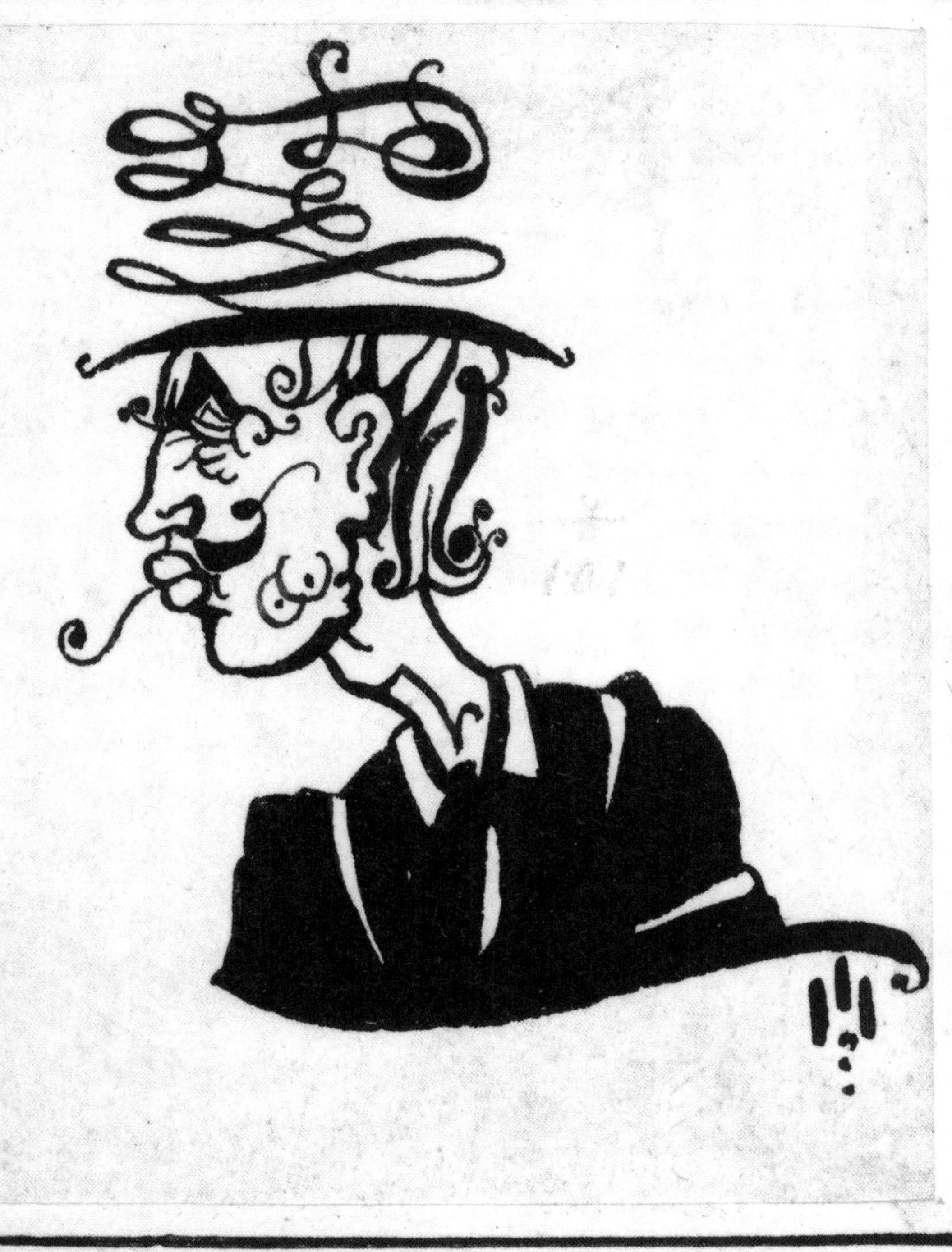

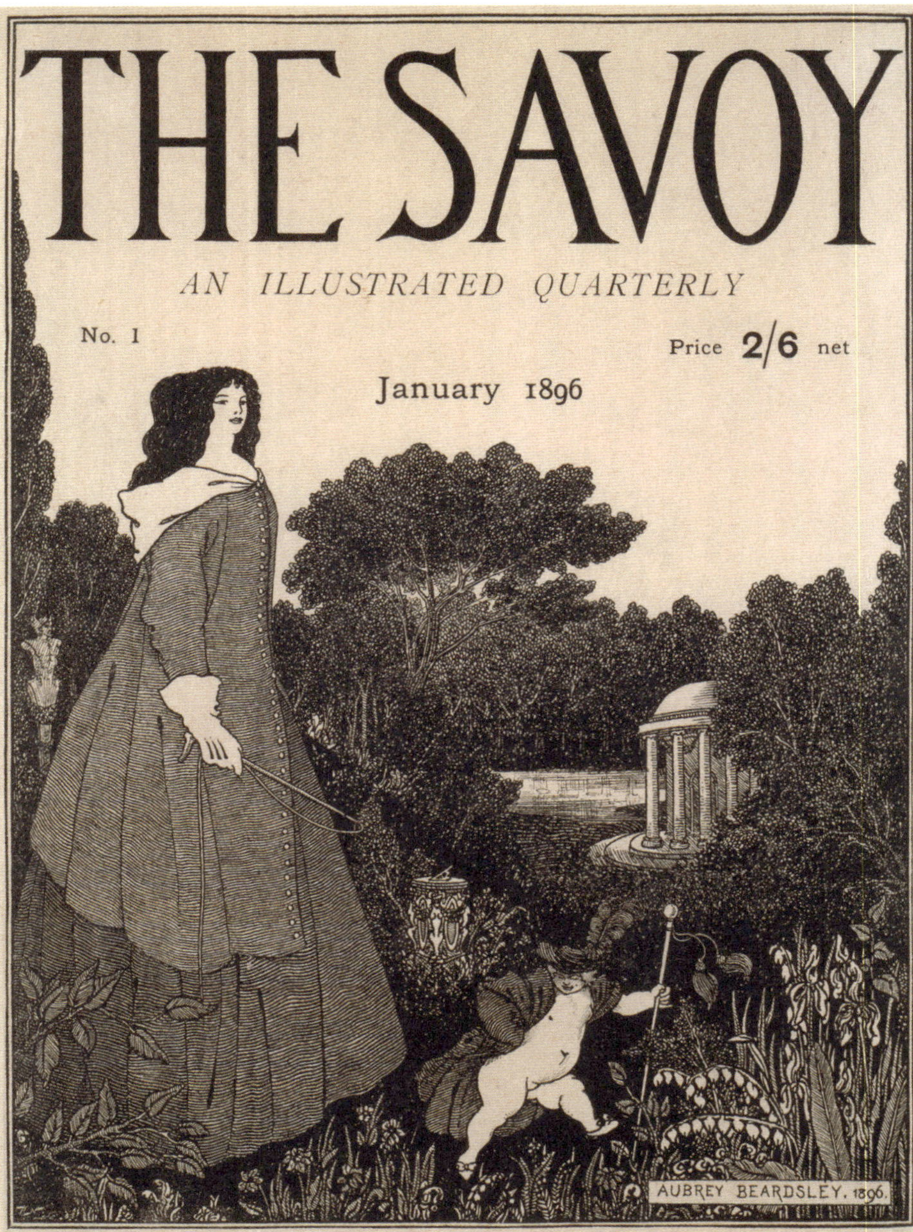
THE SAVOY
AN ILLUSTRATED QUARTERLY
No. 1
Price 2/6 net
January 1896
AUBREY BEARDSLEY. 1896.

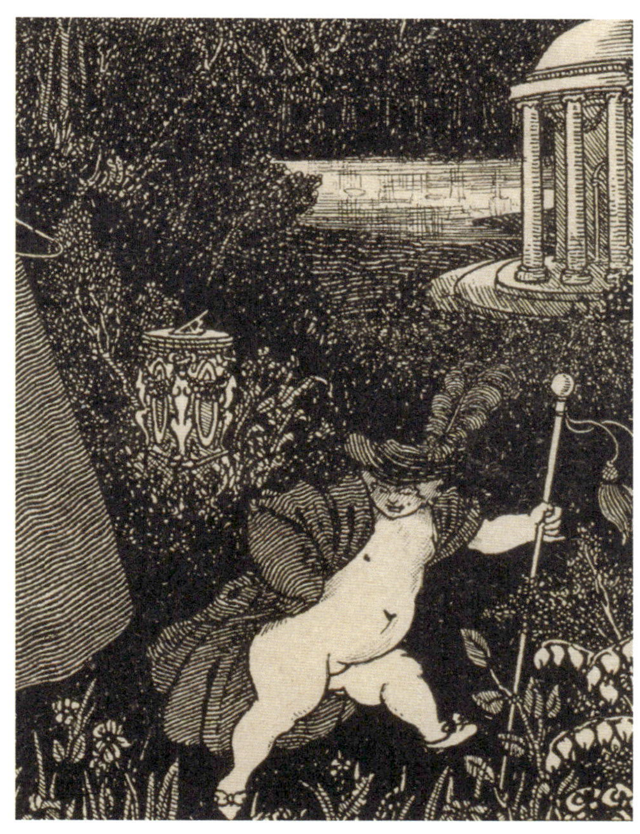

47. Cover of *The Savoy*,
no. 1, January 1896
Line block print
Victoria and Albert Museum, London
(V&A: E.365-1899)

Ousted from *The Yellow Book* after Oscar Wilde's conviction, Beardsley joined forces with the London bookseller Leonard Smithers to produce a new magazine entitled *The Savoy*, which featured a similar mix of literary and pictorial art. His graphic style evolved, to favour rococo and faux-pastoral elements. The mode remained cunningly outrageous: in the original cover design for the first issue, the frock-coated putto was urinating on a *Yellow Book*.

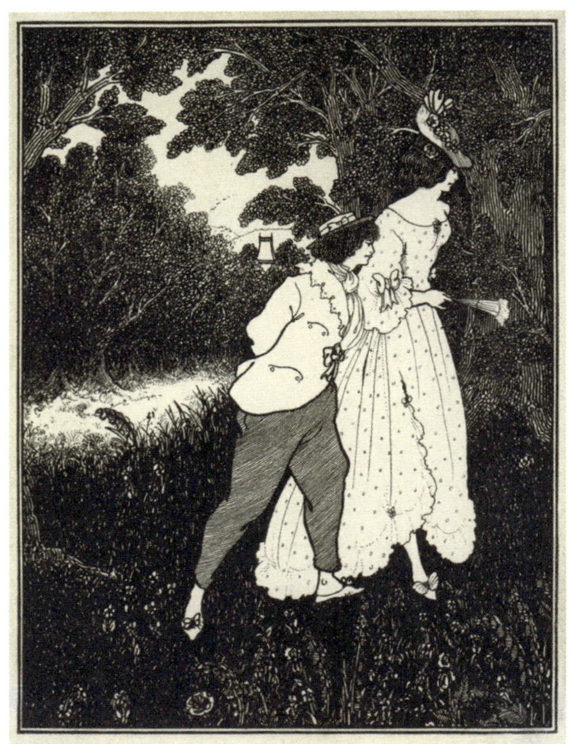

48. *The Three Musicians*, published in *The Savoy*, no. 1, January 1896
Line block print
Victoria and Albert Museum, London (V&A: E.445-1899)

Beardsley also wrote fiction and verse. This image was drawn for his poem in which musicians 'stroll along the path that skirts the wood'. One is a soprano 'lightly frocked in cool white muslin', another 'a slim gracious boy', here resembling a woman dressed as a man, and the third (unpictured) 'a Polish pianist with shocks and shoals of yellow hair'.

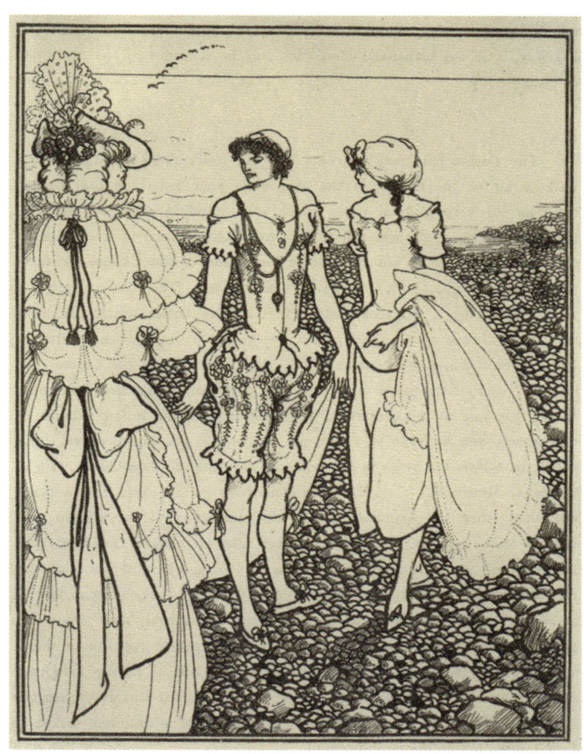

49. *The Bathers / On Dieppe Beach*, published in *The Savoy*, no. 1, January 1896
Line block print
Victoria and Albert Museum, London (V&A: E.444-1899)

The motif of three bathers as female nudes is one used by artists including Renoir and Cezanne, and here Beardsley subverts it with a contemporary twist. *The Savoy* was conceived at Dieppe, where British artists liked to sojourn and about which co-editor Arthur Symons wrote for the magazine, claiming that it was impossible for any woman to look desirable in a bathing dress.[65] So the central figure[66] in this illustration wears 1890s corset underwear, while her companions are clad in time-travelling flounces (left) and a shepherdess costume (right).

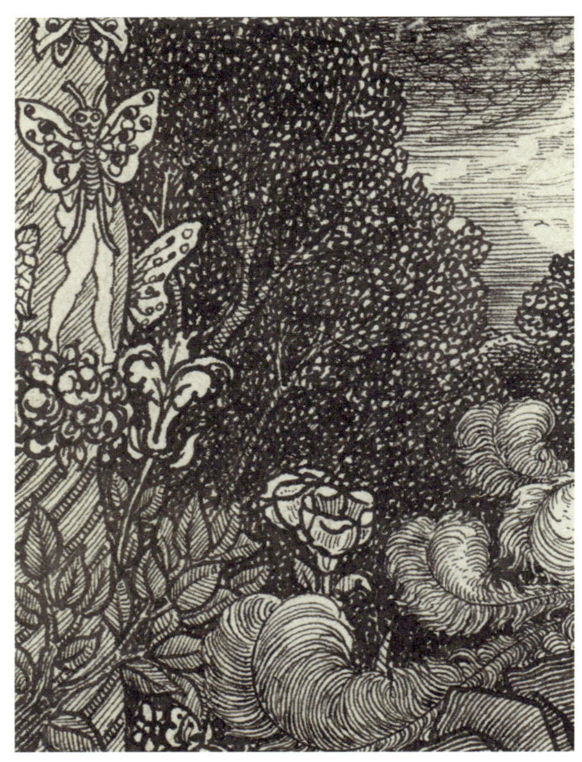

50. *The Abbé (Under the Hill)*,
drawing for illustration to Beardsley's story 'Under the Hill', published in *The Savoy*, no. 1, January 1896
Indian ink on paper
Victoria and Albert Museum, London
(V&A: E.305-1972)

This delicately exquisite image depicts the Abbé Fanfreluche, the hero of Beardsley's grandiloquent, never-finished version of the German legend of Tannhäuser, a composer and poet in search of spiritual enlightenment. As the story opens, Fanfreluche, whose name signifies frills and flounces, stands at 'the sombre gateway of the mysterious Hill, troubled with an exquisite fear lest a day's travel should have too cruelly undone the laboured niceness of his dress'. Both words and image, with its obsessional ink lines, mock Oscar Wilde and all *fin de siècle* dandyism.

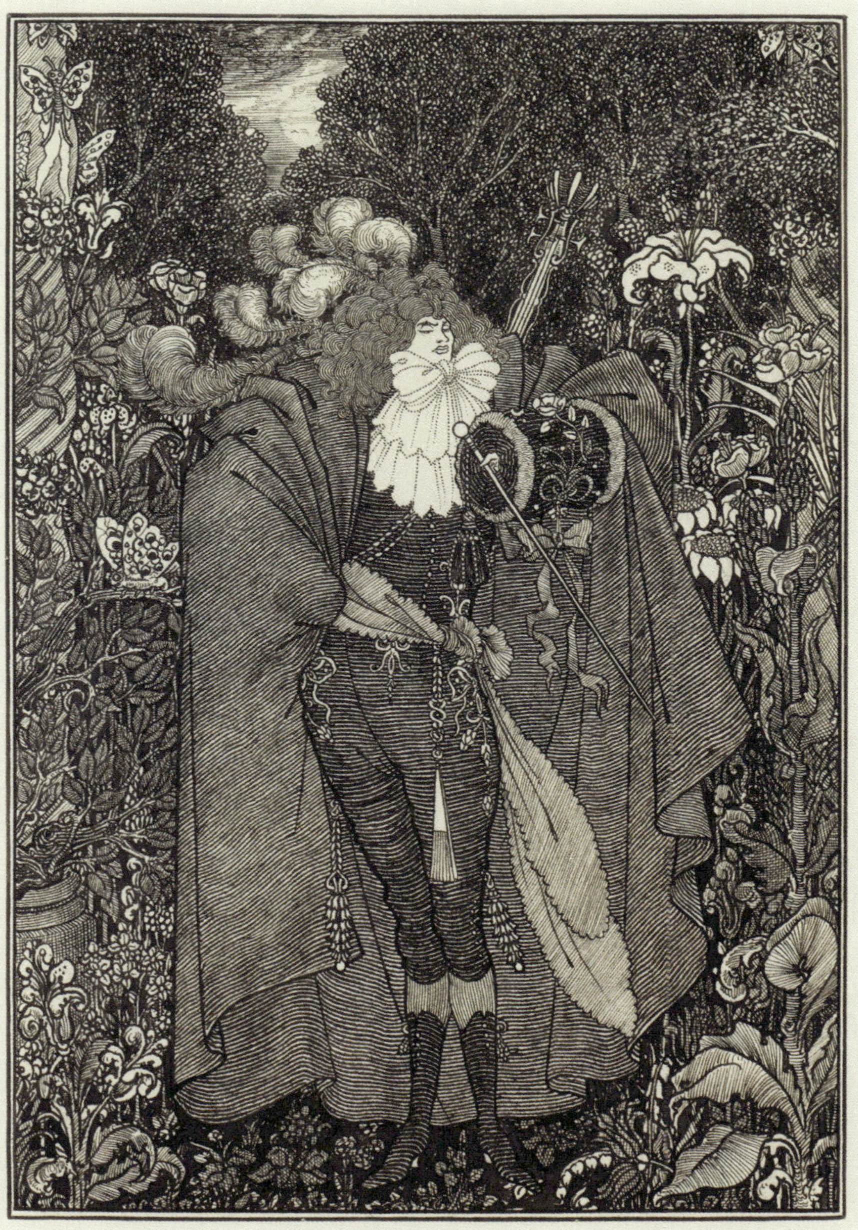

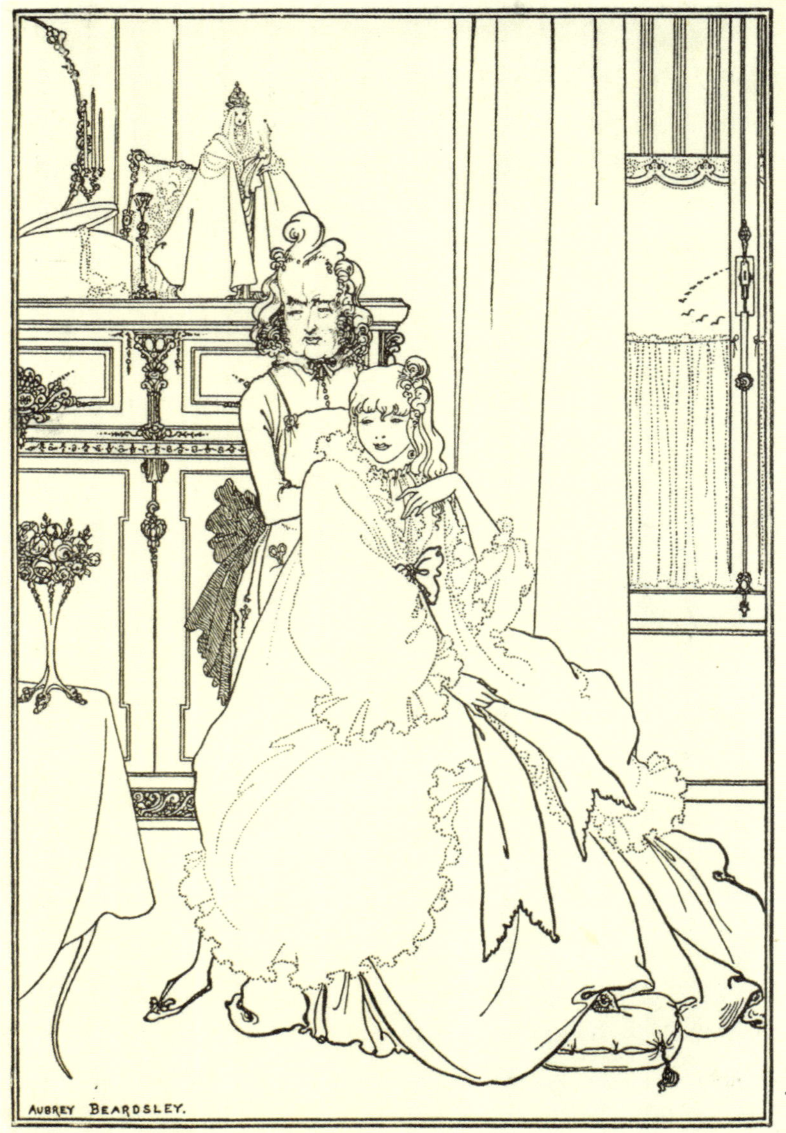
AUBREY BEARDSLEY.

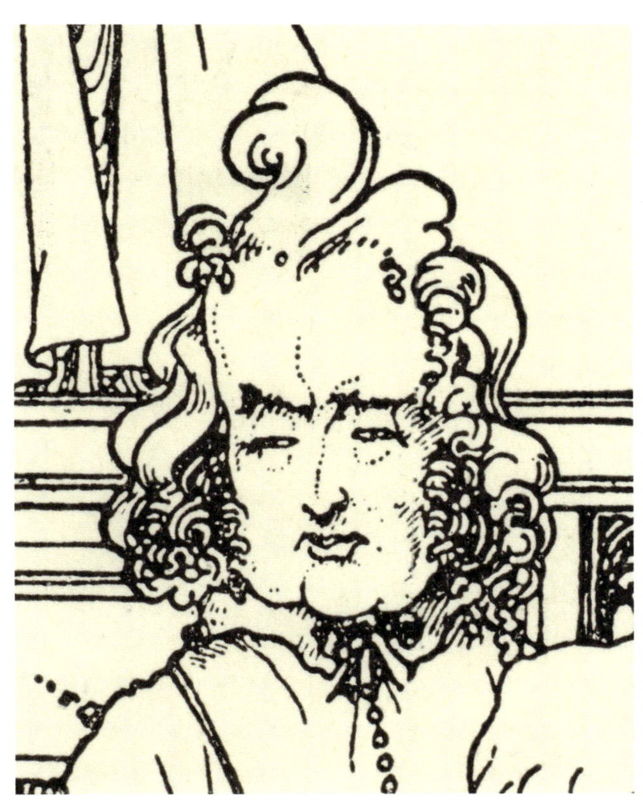

51. *The Coiffing*, published in *The Savoy*, no. 3, March 1896
Line block print
Victoria and Albert Museum, London
(V&A: E.439-1899)

This print illustrates Beardsley's poem *The Ballad of the Barber*, in which a court coiffeur with 'dainty feet' murders a princess whose beauty outshines his cosmetic arts. A long, nervous diagonal line, stretching from the gaze of an Orthodox bishop figurine and the barber's sinister expression, links an asymmetrical composition that holds the ormolu on the cabinet and the lavish lace on the woman's garment in opposition to the vertical lines of wall and window. By this stage, Beardsley's literary aspirations matched his visual ambitions.

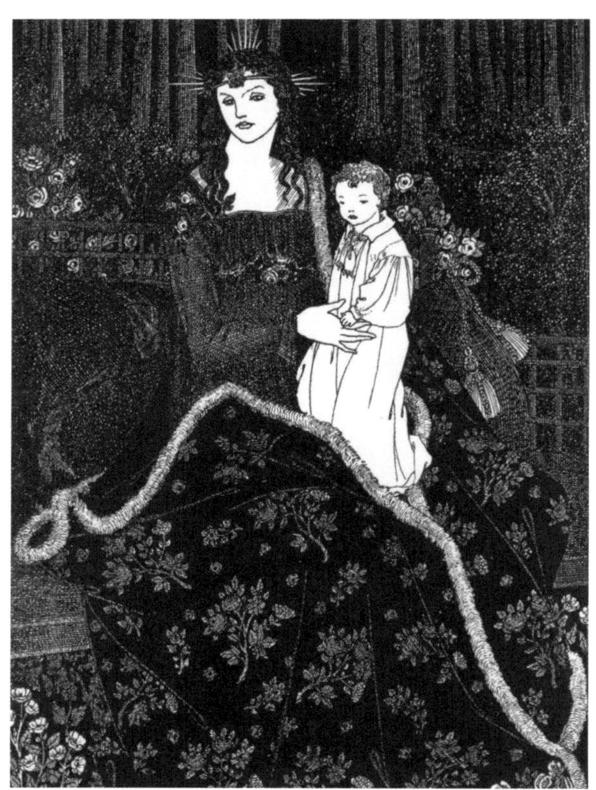

52. A Large Christmas Card, printed insertion for *The Savoy*, no. 1, January 1896
Line block print
Victoria and Albert Museum, London (V&A: E.440-1899)

Drawn and printed as a loose insertion for *The Savoy*, this modern Madonna pays homage to the numerous images of the Virgin Mary and Christ Child in Western art, and the versions that depict them garlanded with flowers. This young mother is wrapped in a fur-trimmed cloak, while her son wears a contemporary nightshirt. Astonishingly chaste compared to *The Savoy*'s provocative designs, it waymarks Beardsley's gradual conversion to Christian beliefs.

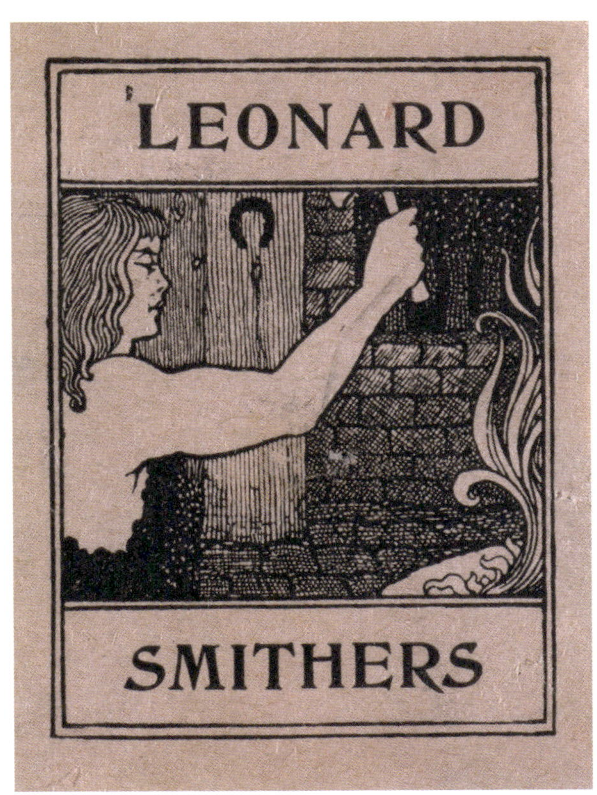

53. *Leonard Smithers*, bookplate, 1890s
Line block print
Victoria and Albert Museum, London
(V&A: E.551-1899)

Overleaf Vignette from *Bon-Mots of Sydney Smith and R. Brinsley Sheridan*, edited by Walter Jerrold and published by J.M. Dent & Co., London, 1893, p. 147
Pen and ink on paper
Victoria and Albert Museum, London
(V&A: E.425-1920)

Stylish personal bookplates became a minor art form in this era. A lawyer-turned-bookseller, with a special interest in classical pornography, Leonard Smithers subsidized *The Savoy*. His bookplate both puns on his name and echoes 'The Forge', a *Savoy* poem by John Gray. Gray was a working-class writer who inspired the homoerotic character Dorian Gray in Oscar Wilde's novel and would promote Beardsley's conversion to the Catholic faith.

'When I go to the theatre, things shape themselves before my eyes just as I draw them ... they all seem weird and strange'

1894

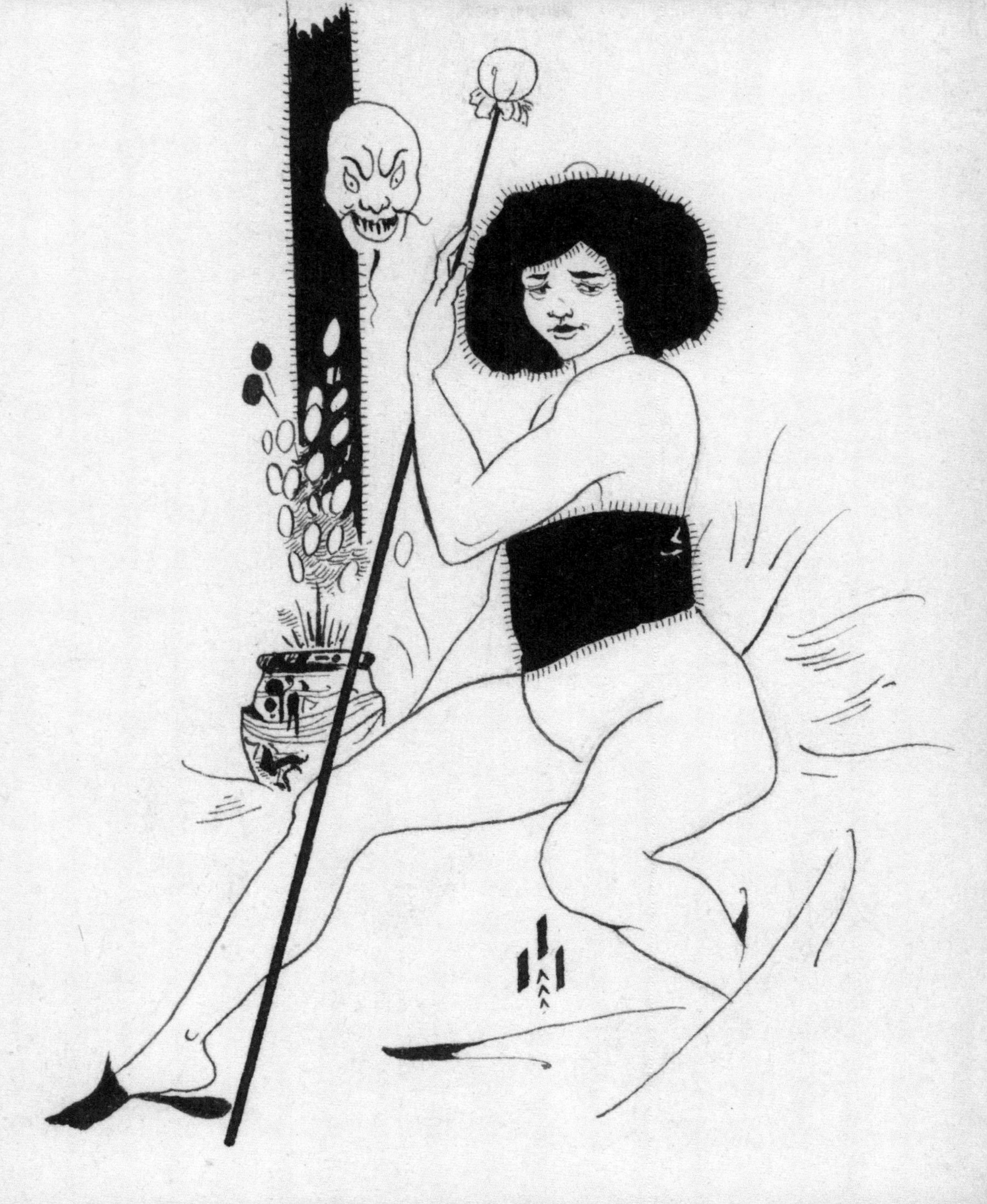

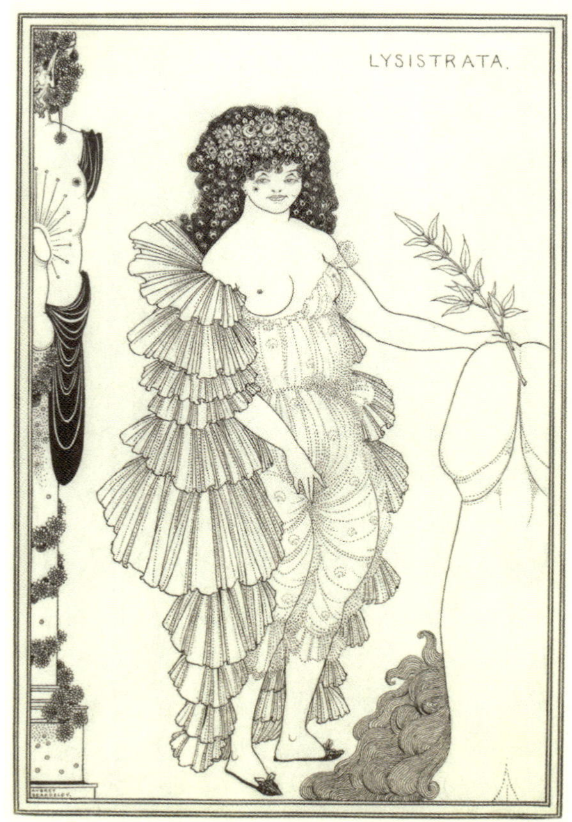

54. *Lysistrata Shielding her Coynte,* drawing for the frontispiece to *Lysistrata,* 1896
Pen and ink over graphite on paper
Victoria and Albert Museum, London
(V&A: E.294-1972)

Leonard Smithers commissioned Beardsley to illustrate the ancient Greek comedy *Lysistrata,* which dramatizes a sex strike campaign by women, led by Lysistrata, to force the men to bring the Peloponnesian War to an end. Characteristically, he combined crude subject matter, often of his own devising, with exquisitely elegant decoration and draughtsmanship. The volume was privately issued to avoid prosecution.

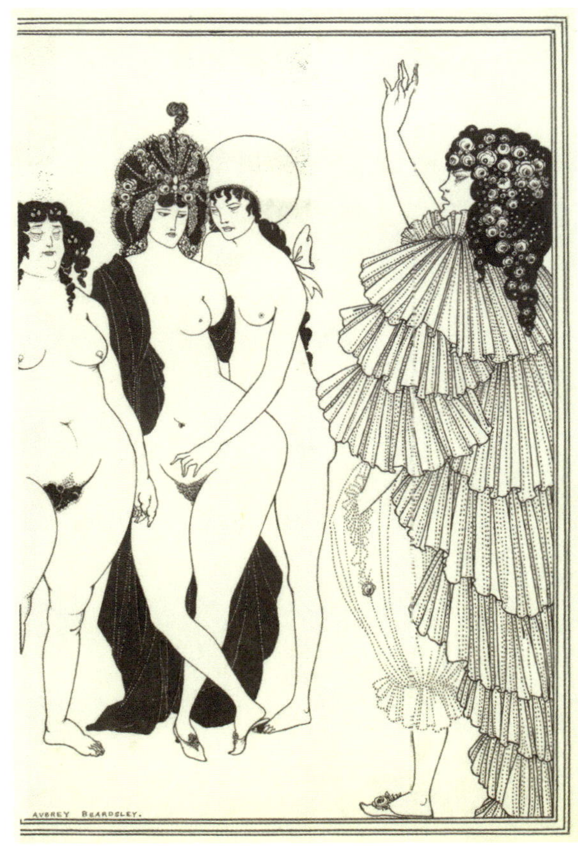

55. Lysistrata Haranguing the Athenian Women, 1896, printed 1929
Pen and ink on paper
Victoria and Albert Museum, London
(V&A: E.296-1972)

'Why do you bite your lips and shake your heads?' Lysistrata demands, urging her fellow Athenians to support the strike. 'We must refrain from every depth of love. Will you or won't you?' Beardsley's fine ink lines erotically satirize the women's bodies, contrasting with Lysistrata's cascade of flounces. Working at great speed, he accomplished almost a drawing a day for the book.

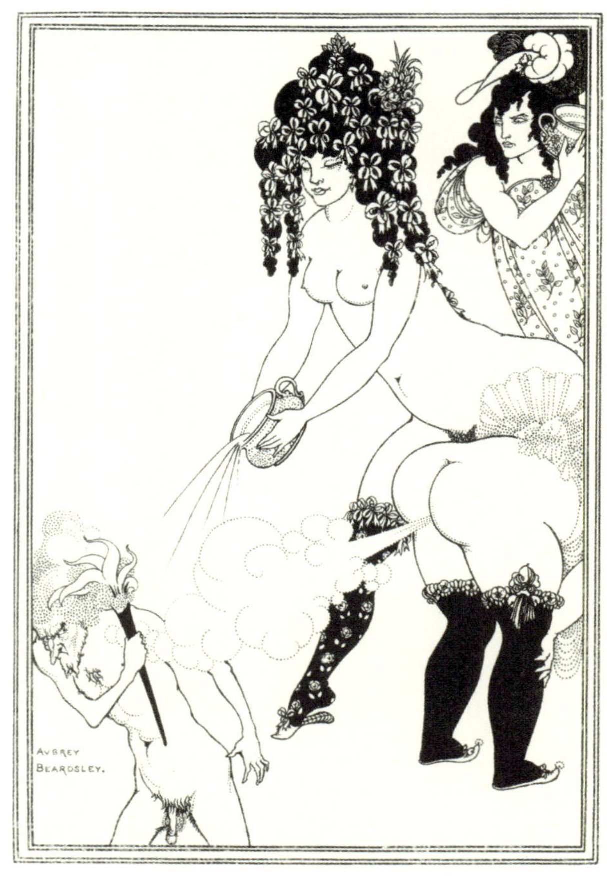

56. *Lysistrata Defending the Acropolis*, 1896
Pen and ink on paper
Victoria and Albert Museum, London
(V&A: E.748-1945)

In Aristophanes' play the women successfully seize and hold the Acropolis against the only men left in Athens, using dirty water as their weapon. The wizened male with his flaming torch is no match for the powerfully stacked scatological female group, while any readerly objections to coarse humour are disarmed by the women's elegant curves and curls.

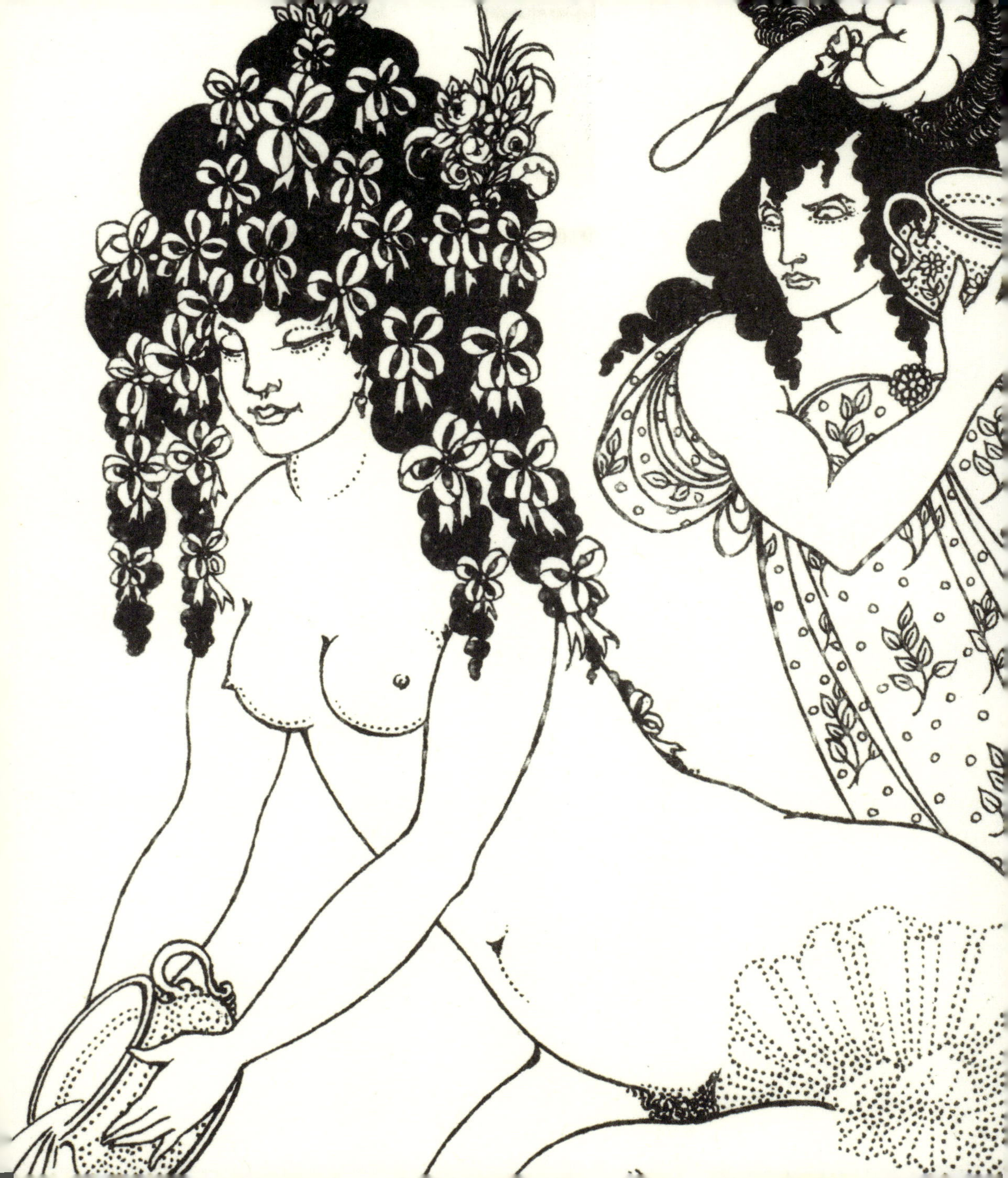

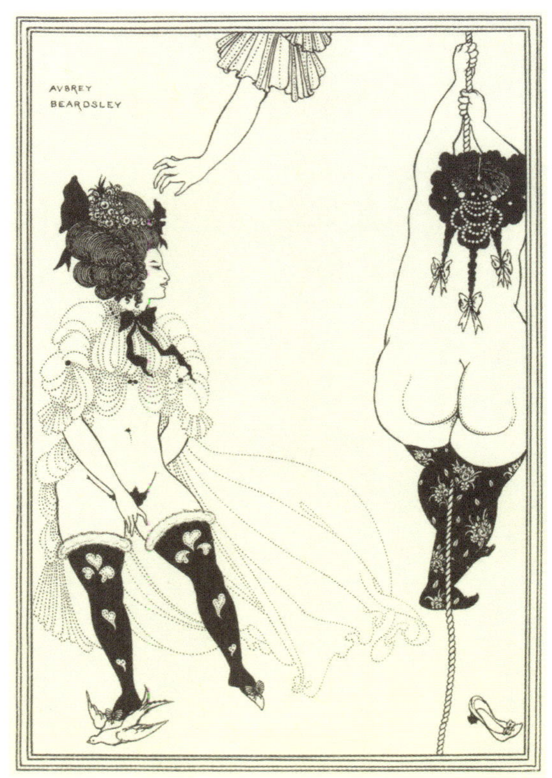

57. Two Athenian Women in Distress, 1896
Collotype print on paper
Victoria and Albert Museum, London
(V&A: E.747-1945)

Borrowing hairstyles and ribbons from erotic eighteenth-century French painting by François Boucher and Jean-Honoré Fragonard, and a linear style from Greek vase painting, Beardsley created astonishing compositions. Here he illustrates those women who attempt to desert the campaign by sliding down a rope or escaping on the back of a bird, as Lysistrata (the arm from above) reaches after them and foils their mutiny. The discarded slipper is a particularly piquant detail.

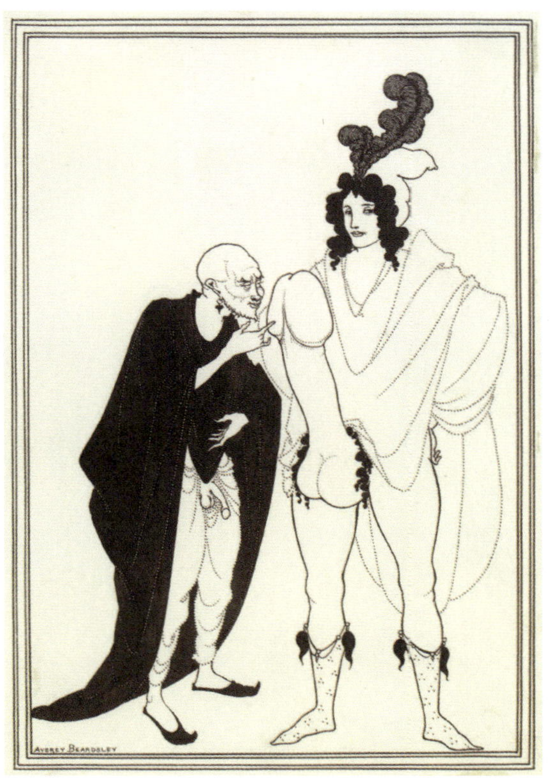

58. *The Examination of the Herald*, 1896
Pen and ink over graphite on paper
Victoria and Albert Museum, London
(V&A: E.300-1972)

With his vivid imagination, Beardsley nonetheless kept to the texts he was illustrating. In Aristophanes' comedy, the messenger from Sparta has an exchange with the Athenian magistrate which is full of lewd allusions. The erect, outsize penis depicted, which forms a major iteration in Beardsley's pictorial commentary, is inspired partly by those in Japanese *shunga* prints, partly by traditional male anxieties, and partly by the enormous phalluses worn by comedic actors in ancient Greek theatre.

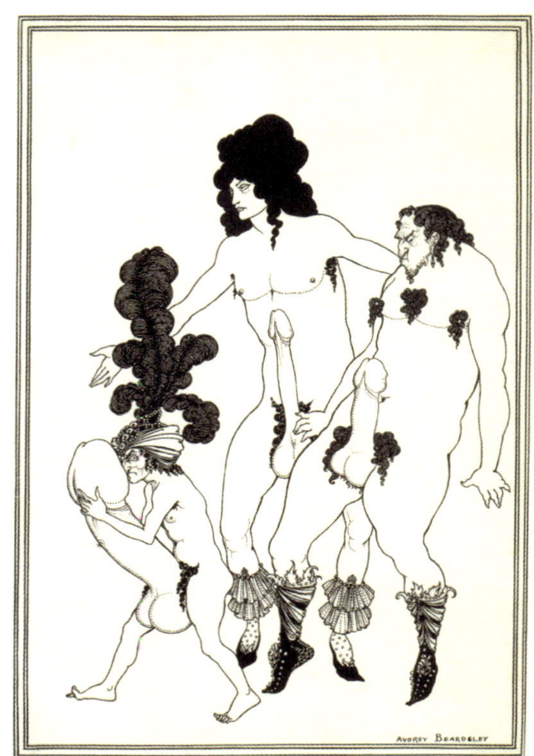

59. *The Lacedaemonian Ambassadors*, 1896
Pen and ink over graphite on paper
Victoria and Albert Museum, London
(V&A: E.301-1972)

Three ambassadors from the city state of Sparta (known in antiquity as Lacedaemonia), in the throes of extreme sexual frustration, arrive to conclude peace talks with Athens under Lysistrata's supervision. Referencing both the ancient Greek theatrical tradition whereby actors wore stage-prop phalluses and the phallic graffiti found on walls and doors from antiquity onwards, the comic spirit of Beardsley's schoolboy drawings is revived in this series, 'mixed with a controlled aggression delivered against both sexes'.[67]

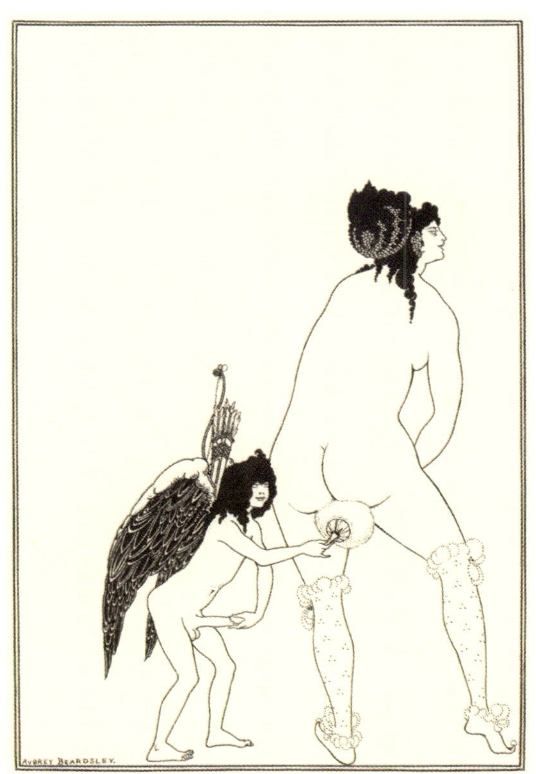

60. *The Toilet of Lampito*, 1896
Pen and ink on paper
Victoria and Albert Museum, London
(V&A: E.295-1972)

Overleaf Vignette from *Bon-Mots of Charles Lamb and Douglas Jerrold*, edited by Walter Jerrold and published by J.M. Dent & Co., London, 1893, p. 108
Pen and ink on paper
Victoria and Albert Museum, London
(V&A: E.325-1972)

In Aristophanes' comedy, Lampito is Lysistrata's Spartan ally. The purchasers of Smithers's privately printed edition were all male, with a classical education, who in their clubs and smoking rooms could laugh and joke at Beardsley's salacious yet graphically refined images. Beardsley wrote in July 1896: 'I think they are in a way the best things I have ever done. They will be printed in pale purple.'[68]

'The keynote of my pictures is pose and attitude'

1895

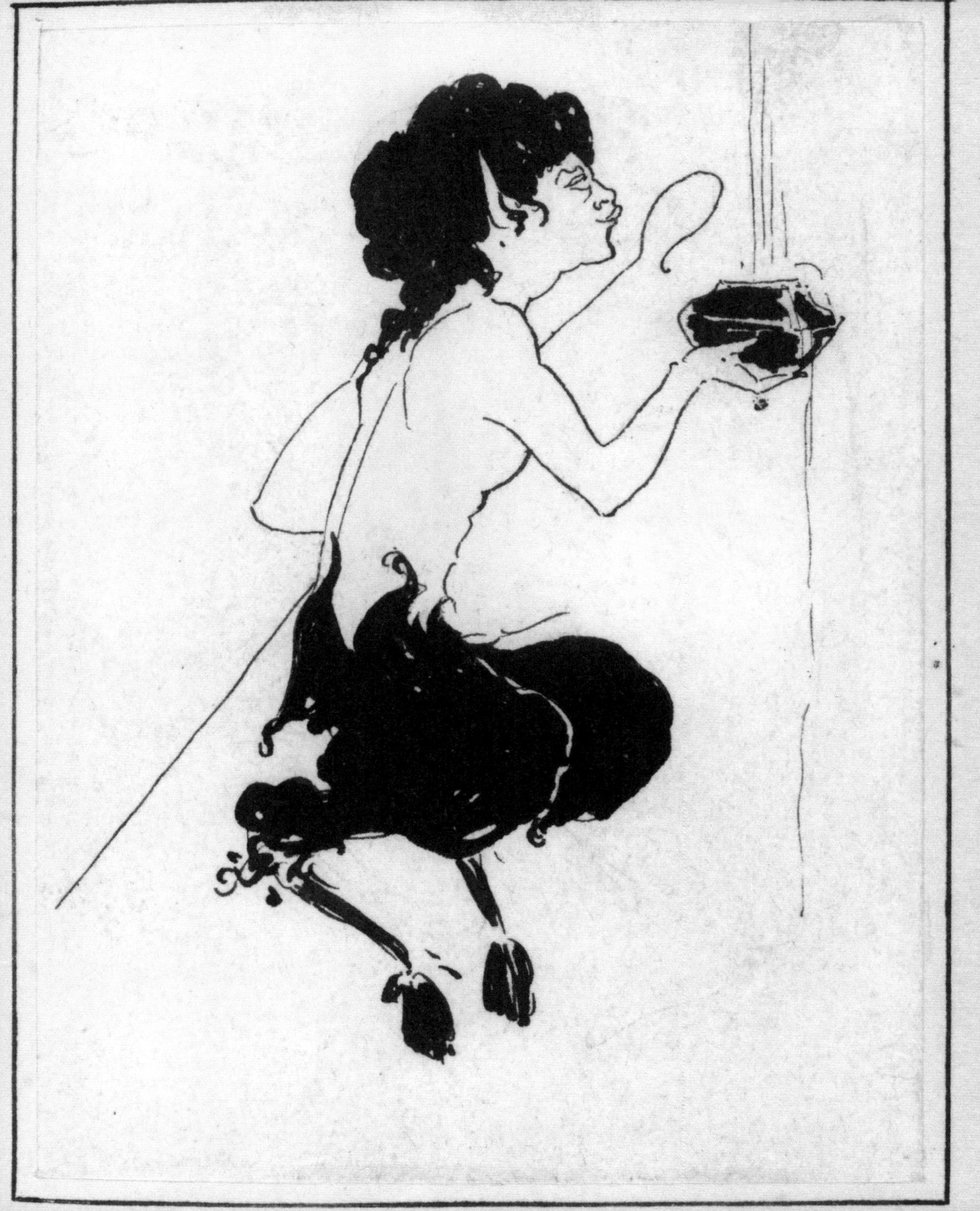

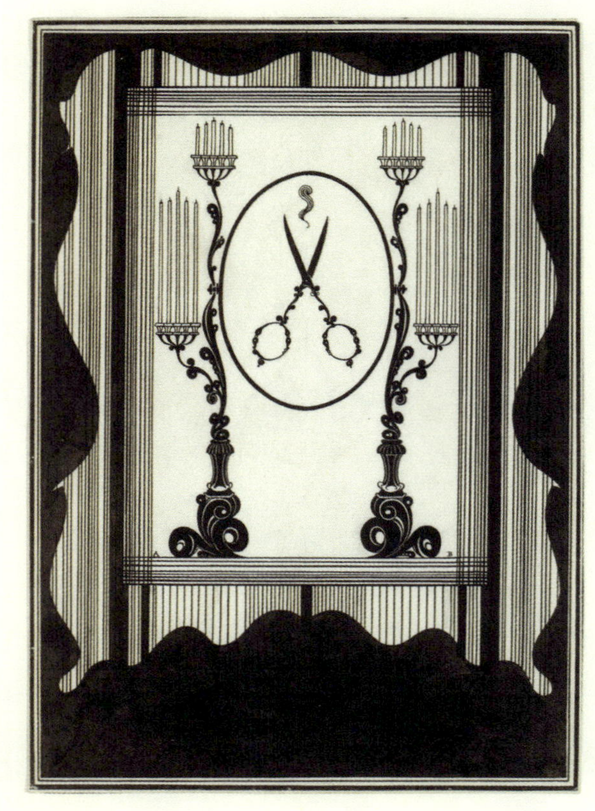

61. Cover design for *The Rape of the Lock* by Alexander Pope, published by Leonard Smithers, London, 1896
Pen and ink on paper
Victoria and Albert Museum, London (V&A: E.304-1972)

The commission to illustrate Alexander Pope's 1712 satirical epic allowed Beardsley to indulge his passion for rococo decoration. First issued as a miniature book, the 1896 edition had an unusually severe cover design, its Neoclassical lines framing the fatal scissors and the small, snipped curl of hair that forms the mock-heroic subject of the poem.

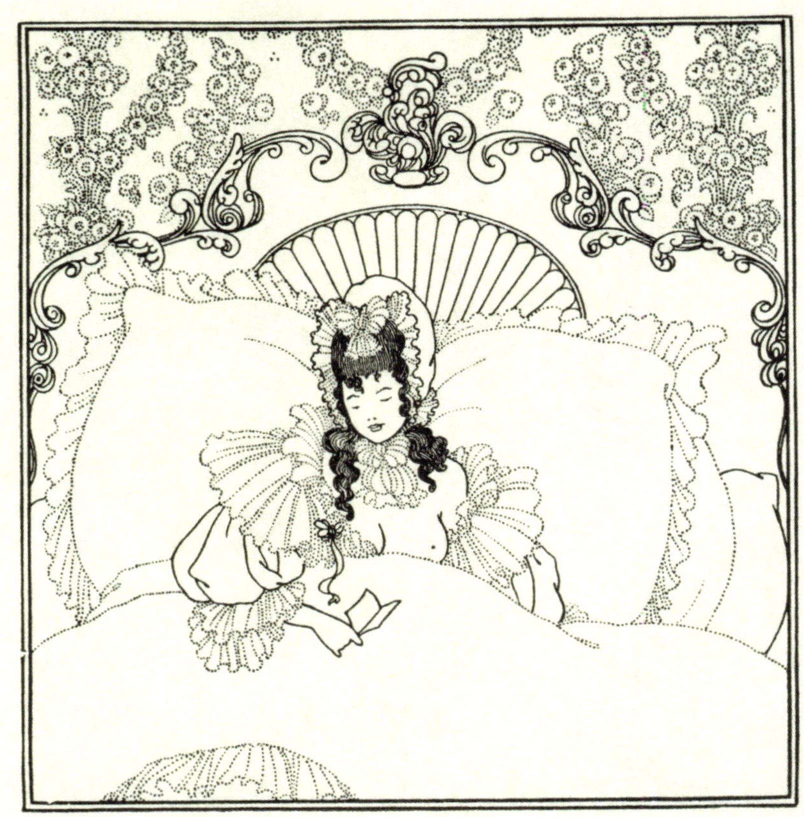

62. *The Billet-Doux*, headpiece to the first canto of *The Rape of the Lock*, 1896; plate 96 to *The Later Work of Aubrey Beardsley*, published by John Lane of The Bodley Head, London, 1901
Line block print on paper
Victoria and Albert Museum, London (V&A: E.752-1987)

Finely stippled line and lacy, filigree patterning establish a polite context for the images and for Pope's poem, which in an extended humorous allegory about stealing a lock of hair tells of the actual rape of the lady Belinda by the vicious Baron. As elsewhere in Beardsley's illustrations for the verse, mischievous details knowingly convey this camouflaged narrative for sophisticated readers.

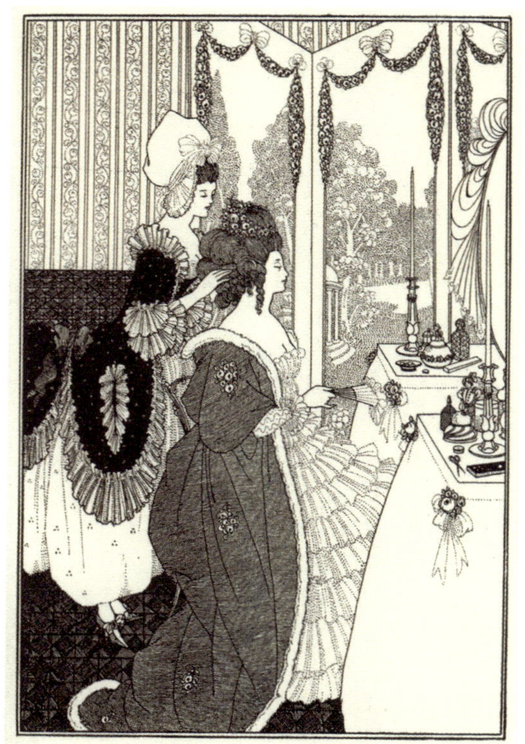

63. *Belinda at her Toilette*, from *The Rape of the Lock* by Alexander Pope, second edition published by Leonard Smithers, London, 1897
Line block print on paper
Royal Academy of Arts
(RA: 12/692)

For Pope's lines describing Belinda's beauty routine as 'the sacred rites of pride', during which Belinda and her lady's maid carefully construct her appearance, Beardsley crafts a densely artificial image. He uses a *shunga*-style mix of patterns with elaborate details of dress and cosmetic jars, and a disorienting background view that may or may not be an angled window or a folding screen. Nothing is at face value.

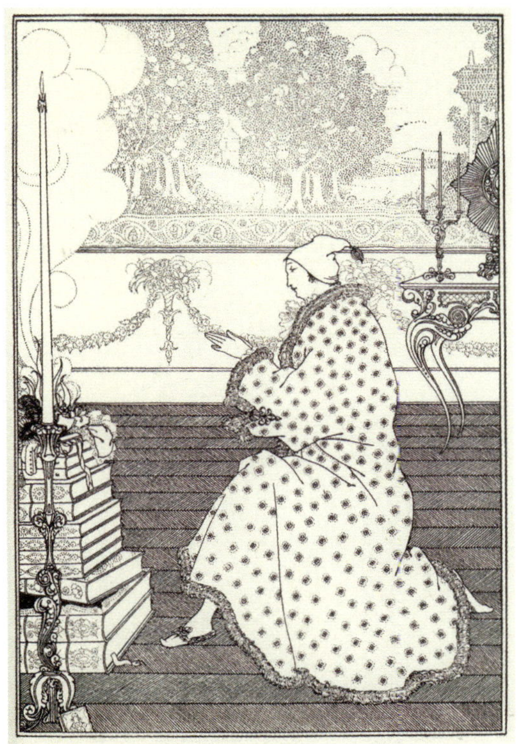

64. *The Baron's Prayer*, from *The Rape of the Lock* by Alexander Pope, second edition published by Leonard Smithers, London, 1897
Line block print on paper
Royal Academy of Arts
(RA 18/607)

Meanwhile, the wicked Baron, in spotted dressing gown and Hogarthian nightcap, also has a shrine, in his case laden with spoils:

> There lay three garters, half a pair of gloves
> And all the trophies of his former loves.
> With tender billet-doux he lights the pyre,
> And breathes three amorous sighs to raise the fire.
> Then prostrate falls, and begs with ardent eyes
> Soon to obtain, and long possess the prize.

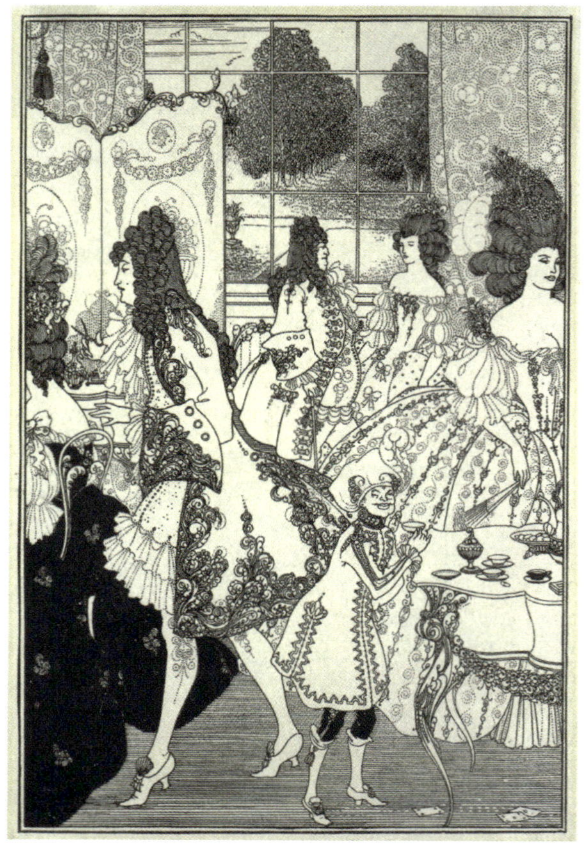

65. *The Deed*, from *The Rape of the Lock* by Alexander Pope, second edition published by Leonard Smithers, London, 1897
Line block print
Victoria and Albert Museum, London (V&A: E.426-1899)

Amid the decorative patterning of embroidered garments, together with a wave of tall wigs that echo the leafy trees beyond, it is hard to discern the scissors as the Baron (left) creeps up behind the seated Belinda, only half in the picture. This 'off-scene' positioning stands for the violent act encoded in snipping a lock of luxuriant hair. In the foreground a grotesque pageboy grins at the spectator.

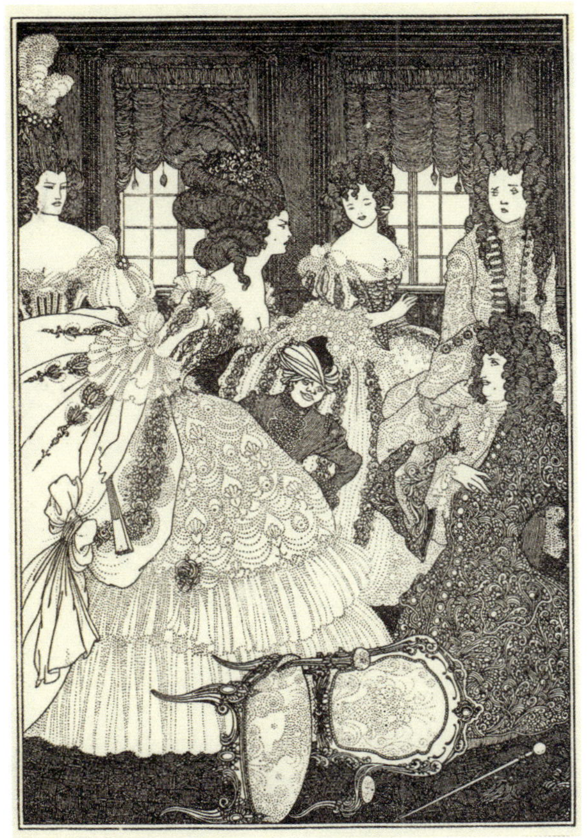

66. *The Battle of the Beaux and the Belles*, from *The Rape of the Lock* by Alexander Pope, second edition published by Leonard Smithers, London, 1897
Line block print
Victoria and Albert Museum, London (V&A: E.437-1899)

'To arms! To arms!' cries Belinda, leading the attack on the Baron. 'Fans clap, silks rustle, whalebones crack', and the Baron falls victim to a charge of snuff. Beardsley's dotting, stippling and hatching yield the half-tone shading of old-style copper engraving. On seeing these images for *The Rape of the Lock*, Whistler declared: 'Aubrey, I have made a very great mistake – you are a very great artist.'[69]

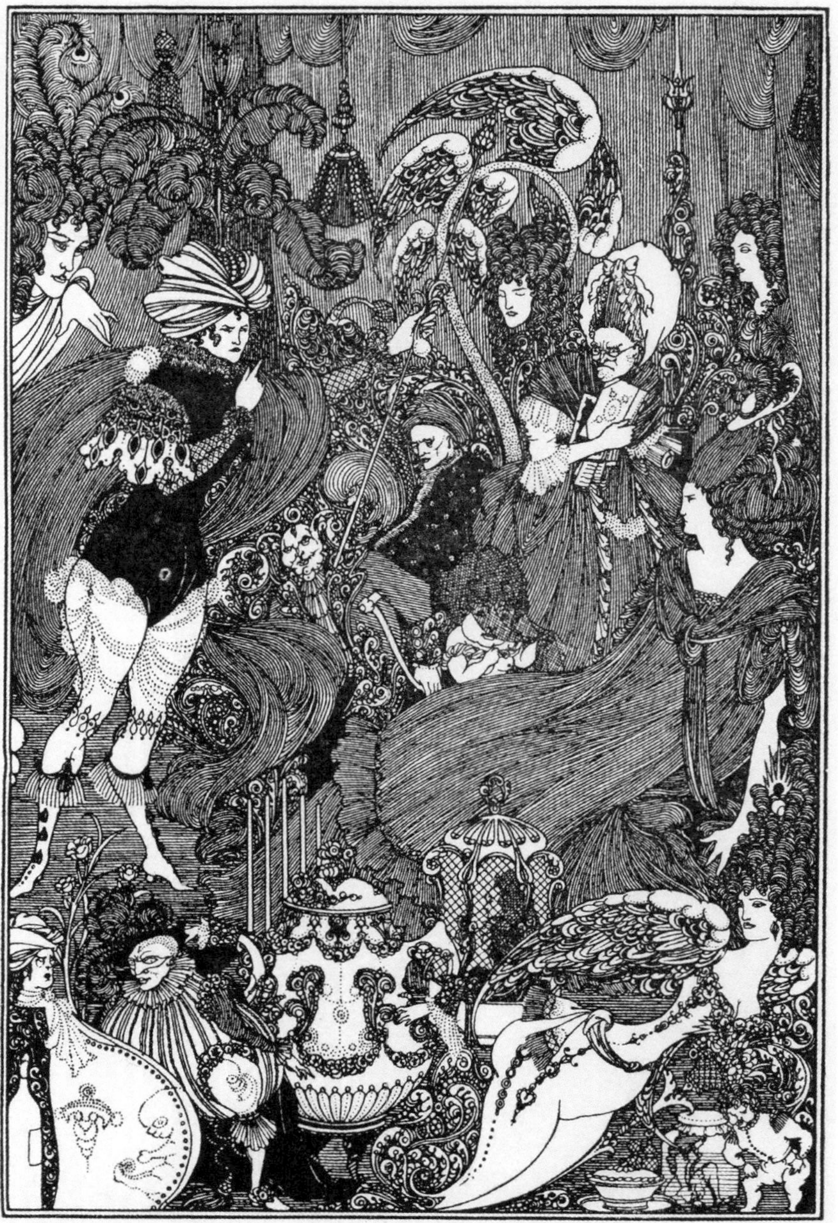

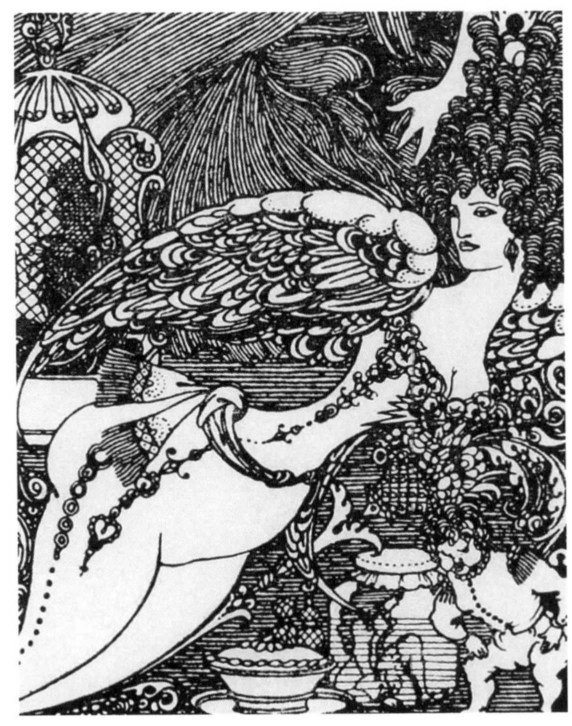

67. *The Cave of Spleen*, from *The Rape of the Lock* by Alexander Pope, second edition published by Leonard Smithers, London, 1897
Line block print on paper
Royal Academy of Arts
(RA: 18/615)

The 'rage, resentment and despair' Belinda feels for her 'ravish'd hair' are represented in verse by a mock-epic descent into a grotesque underworld, where

> Unnumber'd Throngs, on ev'ry side are seen
> Of Bodies chang'd to various forms by Spleen …
> A Pipkin there like Homer's Tripod walks;
> Here sighs a Jar, and there a Goose-pye talks.

Beardsley's hellish scene holds some 15 sour, splenetic figures, more sinister than comic.

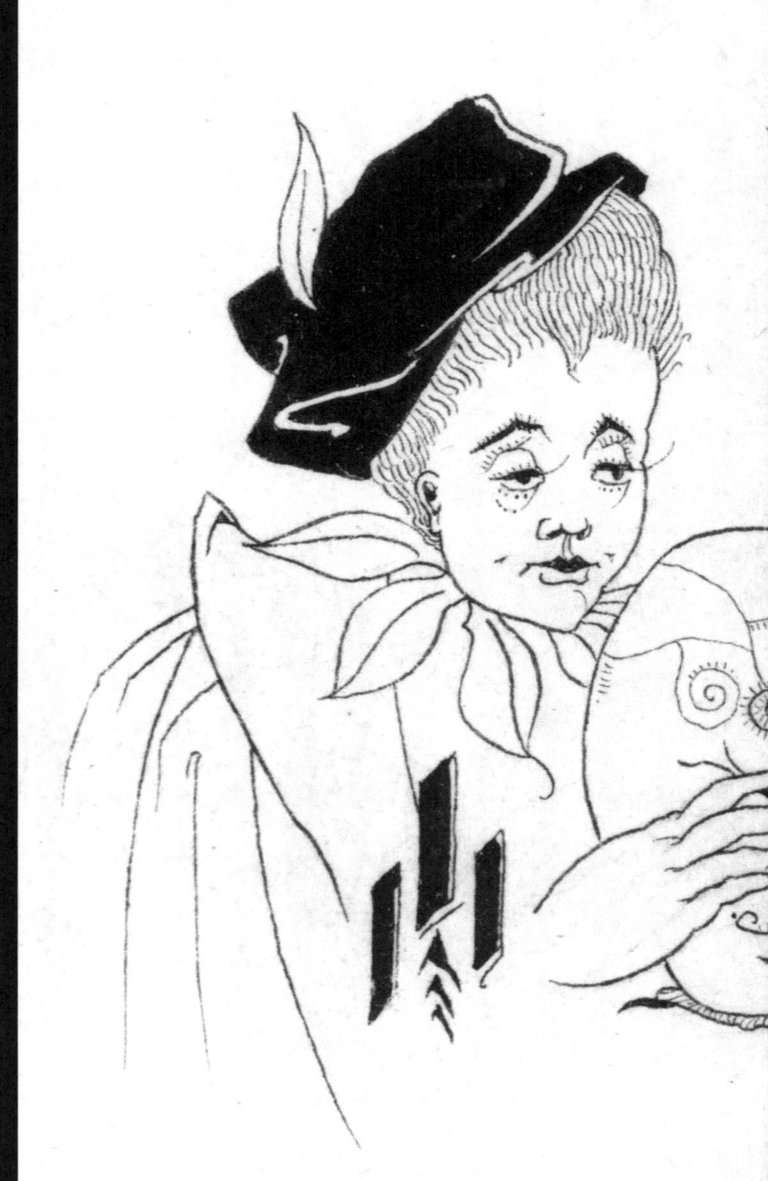

Vignette from *Bon-Mots of Sydney Smith and R. Brinsley Sheridan*, edited by Walter Jerrold and published by J.M. Dent & Co., London, 1893, p. 26
Pen and ink on paper
Victoria and Albert Museum, London
(V&A: E.314-1972)

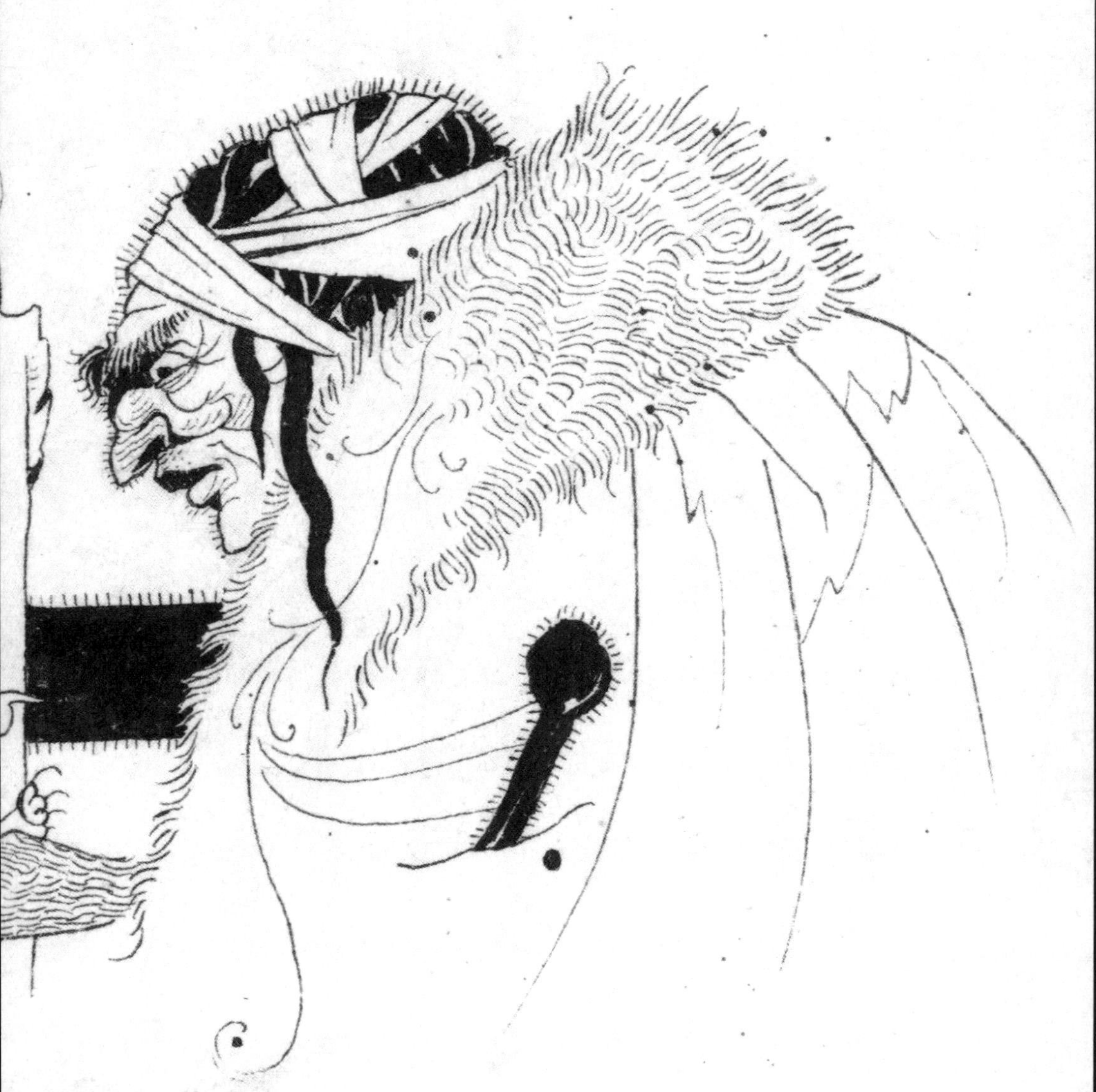

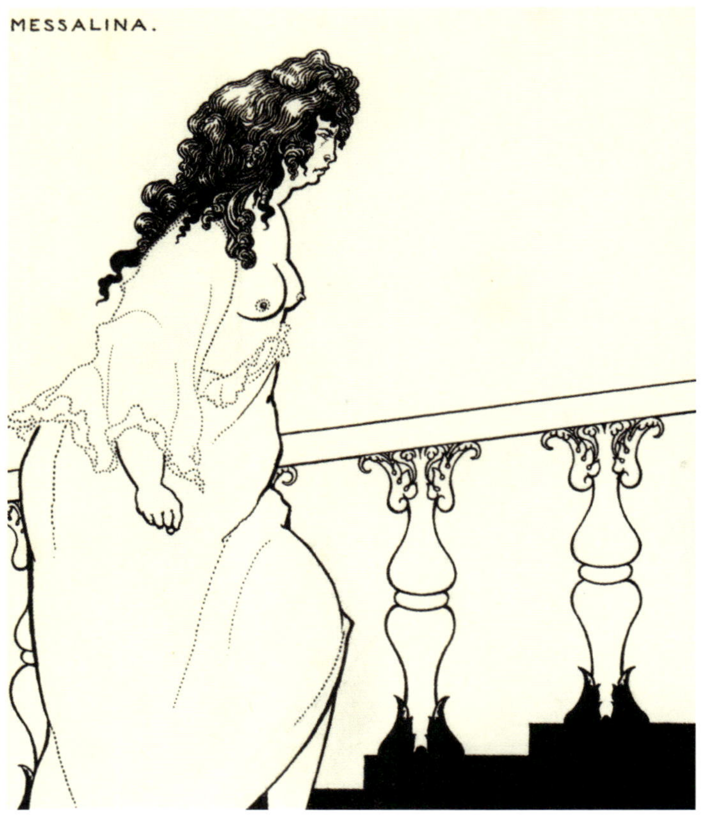

68. *Messalina Returning Home*, illustration for the *Sixth Satire of Juvenal*, 1896, published by Leonard Smithers in *Five Drawings Illustrative of Juvenal and Lucian*, London, 1906
Pen and ink on paper
Victoria and Albert Museum, London (V&A: E.302-1972)

With his decision to produce illustrations to the satire 'Against Women' by the Roman poet Juvenal, Beardsley allied himself with classical and contemporary misogyny, and in doing so reverted to a starker black-and-white mode. The emperor's wife Messalina was accused by her enemies of nightly visits to a brothel, enjoying sex with all customers before reluctantly returning to the palace. The drawing bespeaks disgust with middle-aged as well as insatiable lust.

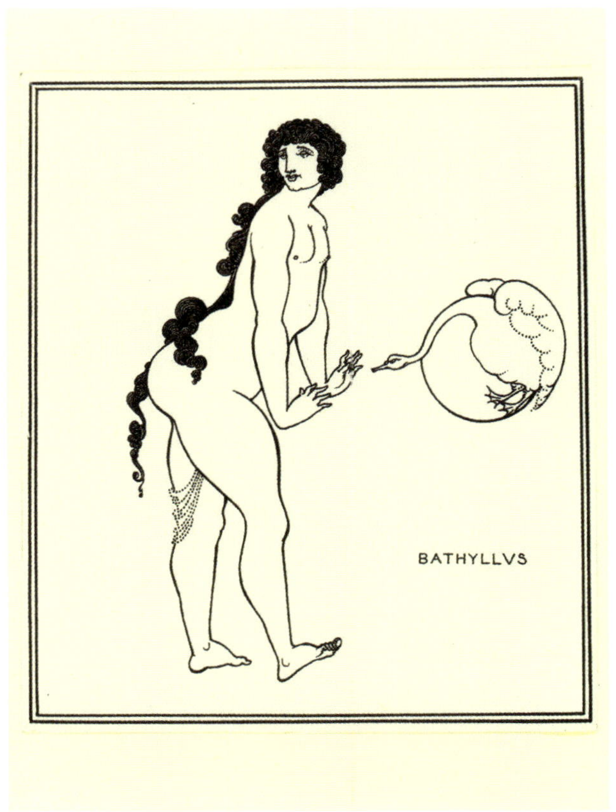

69. *Bathyllus in the Swan Dance*, illustration for the *Sixth Satire of Juvenal*, 1896, published by Leonard Smithers in *Five Drawings Illustrative of Juvenal and Lucian*, London, 1906
Pen and ink on paper
Victoria and Albert Museum, London
(V&A: E.303-1972)

Bathyllus was a Roman actor notorious for his drag performances, whom Beardsley endows with an androgynous, muscular physique. Juvenal alleged that Bathyllus's sexy mime of the maiden Leda's legendary connexion with Jupiter in the shape of a swan was so arousing to female spectators that 'Tuccia wets herself and Apula yelps as if orgasmic'.

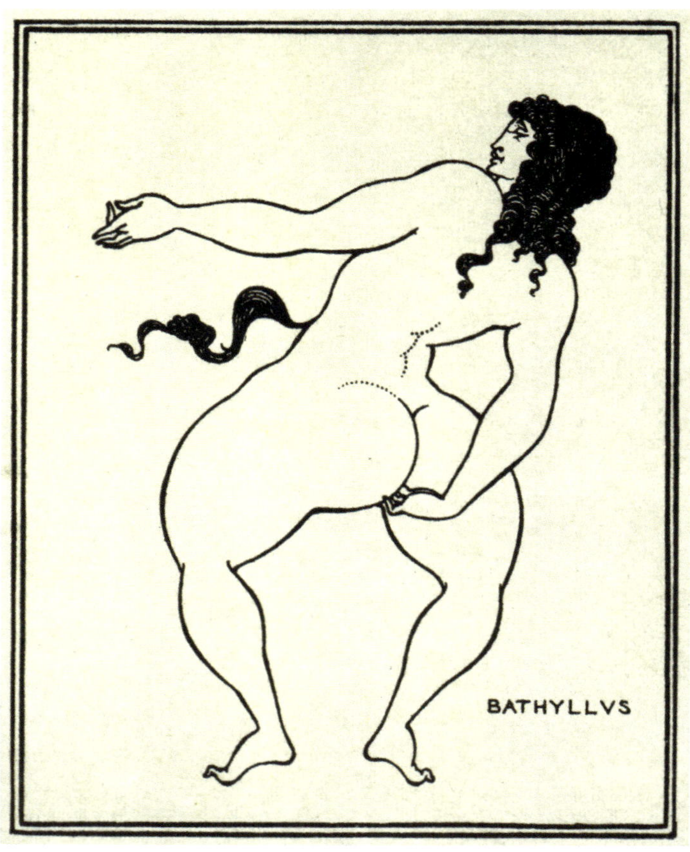

70. *Bathyllus Posturing*, illustration for the *Sixth Satire of Juvenal*, 1896, published by Leonard Smithers in *Five Drawings Illustrative of Juvenal and Lucian*, London, 1906
Pen and ink on paper
Victoria and Albert Museum, London (V&A: E.685-1945)
Given anonymously

In late Victorian Decadent culture, cross-dressing and sexual ambiguity were popular in music-hall acts and high-flown poetry, as rigid binary notions of sexuality were briefly relaxed. Bathyllus became a minor transgender cult figure and Beardsley's depiction of the corpulent performer may contain a coded attack on Oscar Wilde, who had recently been convicted of gross indecency.

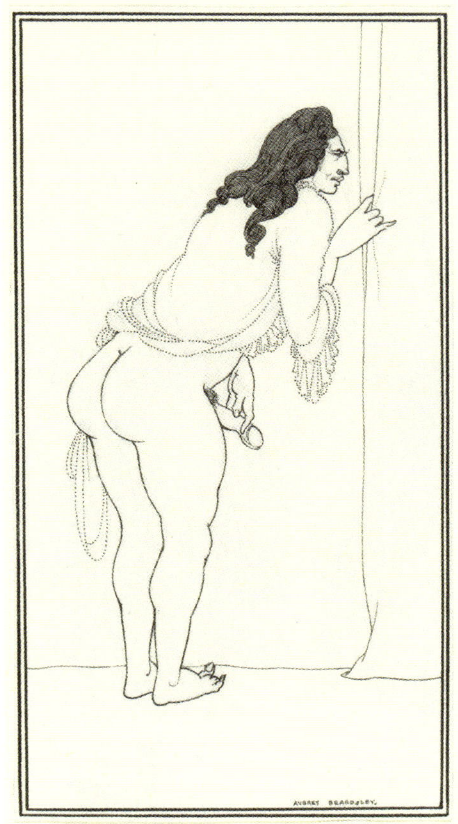

71. *The Impatient Adulterer*, illustration for the *Sixth Satire of Juvenal*, 1896–7, unpublished
Pen and ink over graphite on paper
Victoria and Albert Museum, London
(V&A: E.338-1972)

An especially crude image, this unpublished and now mis-titled figure was intended to illustrate Juvenal's attack on mothers who pimp their daughters. Here a woman's masturbating client is peeping behind curtains while awaiting entry to her daughter's bedroom. In Britain, child prostitution, trafficking and homosexual acts had all been criminalized in 1885.

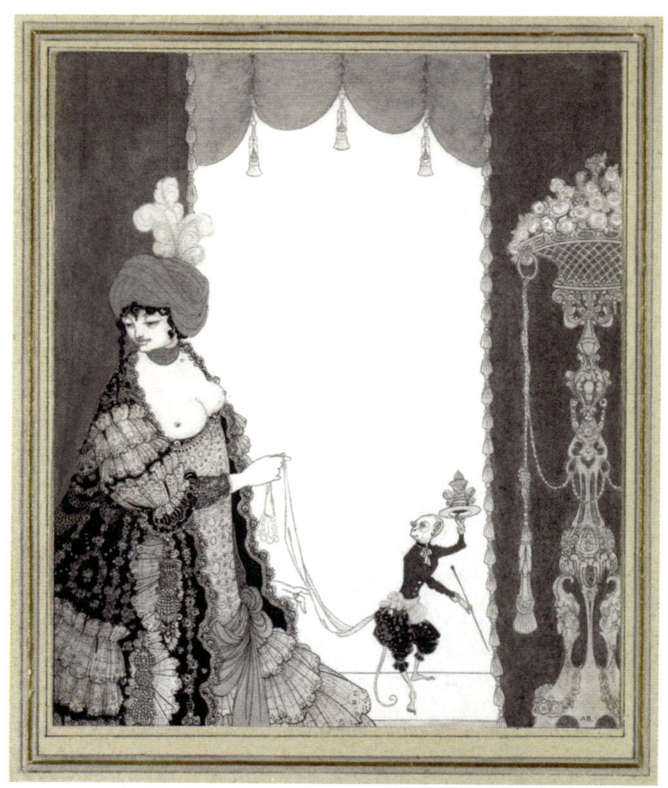

72. *The Lady with the Monkey*, 1897, from *Six Drawings illustrating Théophile Gautier's Romance Mademoiselle de Maupin*, published by Leonard Smithers, London, 1898
Pen, ink and wash on paper
Victoria and Albert Museum, London (V&A: E.308-1972)

Despite or maybe because of his worsening health, Beardsley's ambitions flourished in 1897. His sophisticated half-tone illustrations to the cult novel *Mademoiselle de Maupin* by Gautier expressed both Aesthetic theory and transgender sexual fantasies, while also riffing on caprice; as Gautier's text describes the cross-dressing Rosalind in *As You Like It*, 'affected, inconstant, prudish, languorous, she was everything by turns … An imp, a monkey, and an attorney in conjunction could have invented no more mischievous tricks.'

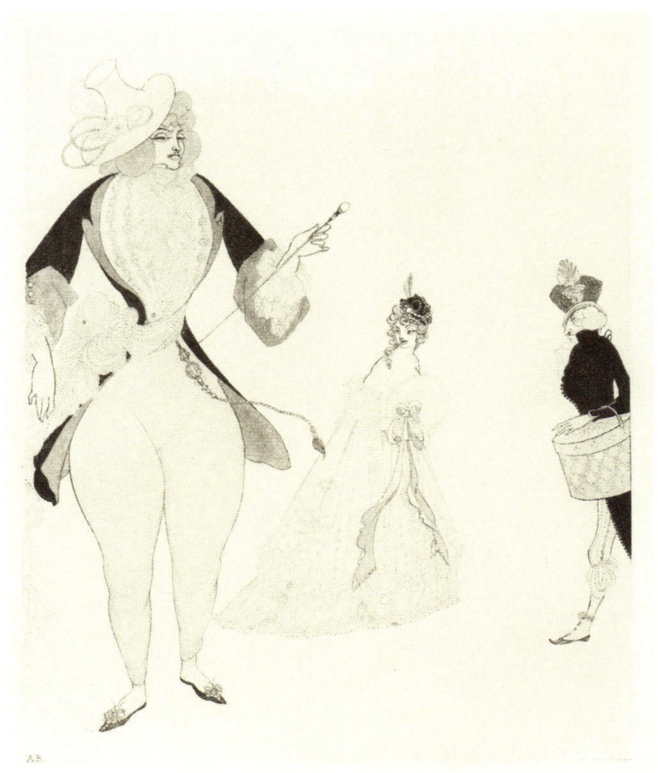

73. *D'Albert in search of his ideal*, 1897, from *Six Drawings illustrating Théophile Gautier's Romance Mademoiselle de Maupin*, published by Leonard Smithers, London, 1898
Photogravure from ink and wash drawing
Victoria and Albert Museum, London (V&A: E.418-1972)
Given by Michael Harari in memory of his father, Ralph A. Harari

Gautier's hero, the chevalier d'Albert, fantasizes about his ideal lover, yet every woman he meets falls short of female perfection. Embarking on an affair with the lovely Rosette, he is thrown into confusion when she receives a handsome young visitor, who arouses unfamiliar passions in d'Albert. The corseted chevalier depicted recalls the decadent Prince Regent and the doomed Oscar Wilde.

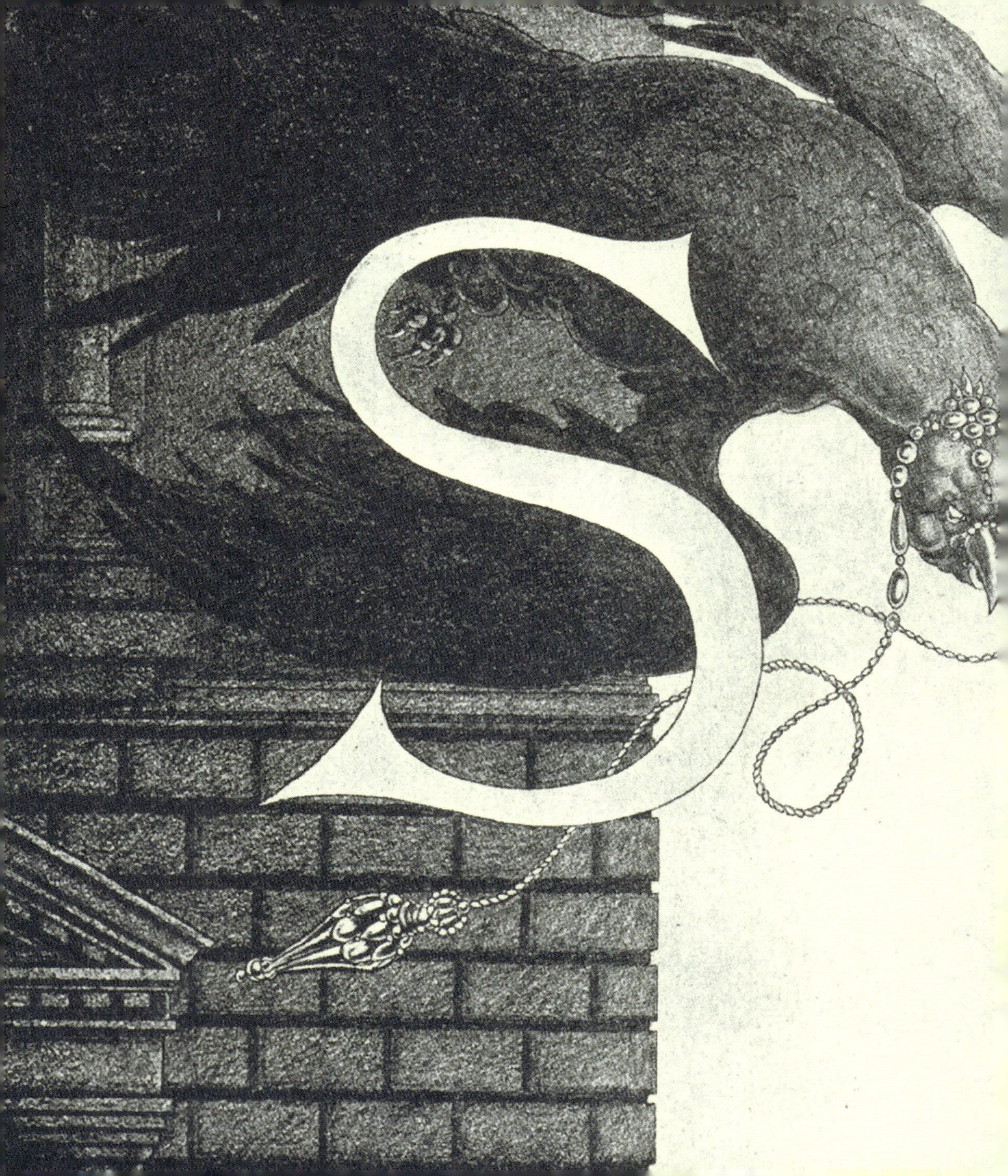

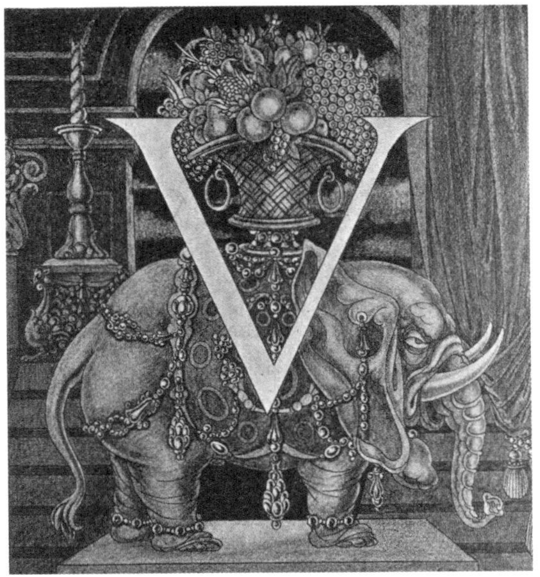

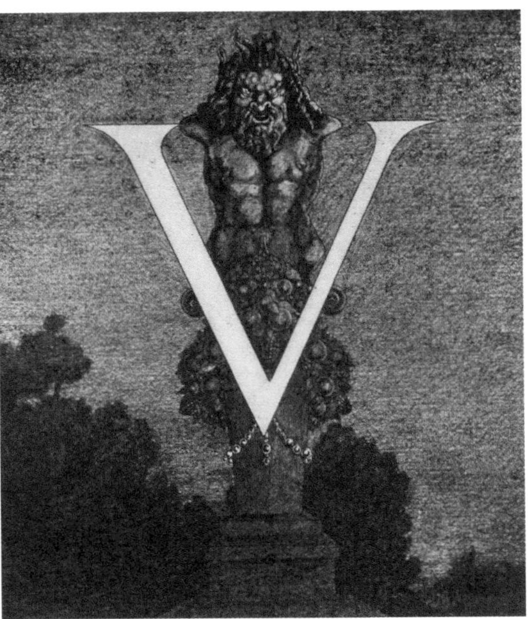

Beardsley's latest graphic manner, half-tone designs for photo-engraving, aimed to reject Victorian medievalism and line drawing in favour of 'a wholesome seventeenth- and eighteenth-century standard of picture making'.[70] He viewed the eponymous miser Volpone in Ben Jonson's Jacobean drama as a 'splendid sinner' whose 'very excess of wickedness'[71] was to be marvelled at. In the decorated initials, the hawk, grinning herm (a pillar with a carved head) and bejewelled elephant illustrate Volpone's rapaciousness, shamelessness and greedy accumulation of wealth.

74. Volpone initial 'S', initial 'V' with herm and initial 'V' with elephant, 1898
Halftone line block prints
Victoria and Albert Museum, London
(V&A: E.1094 to 1096-1996)

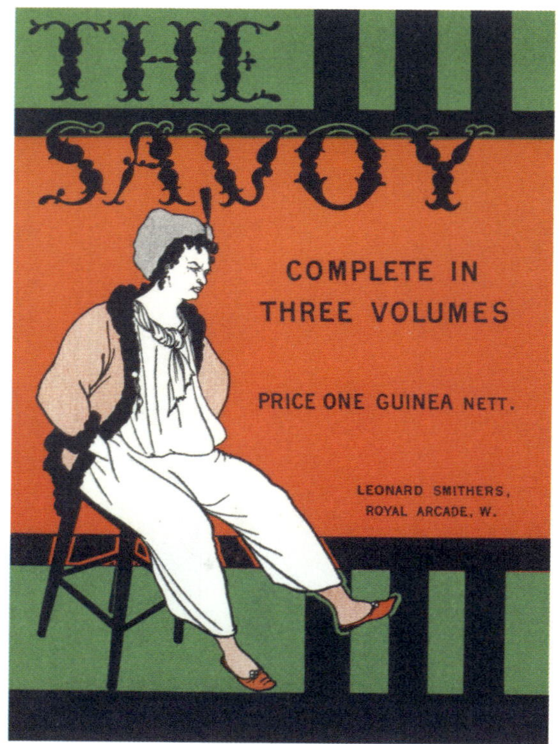

75. Small poster or show-card advertising an edition of *The Savoy*, 1897
Colour lithograph and letterpress
Victoria and Albert Museum, London
(V&A: E.446-1965)

Originally a plain design for issue 8 of *The Savoy*, showing an ambiguous figure in quasi-oriental dress, with sulky posture and expression, this was re-purposed and coloured as a showcard advertising a collected edition of the magazine.

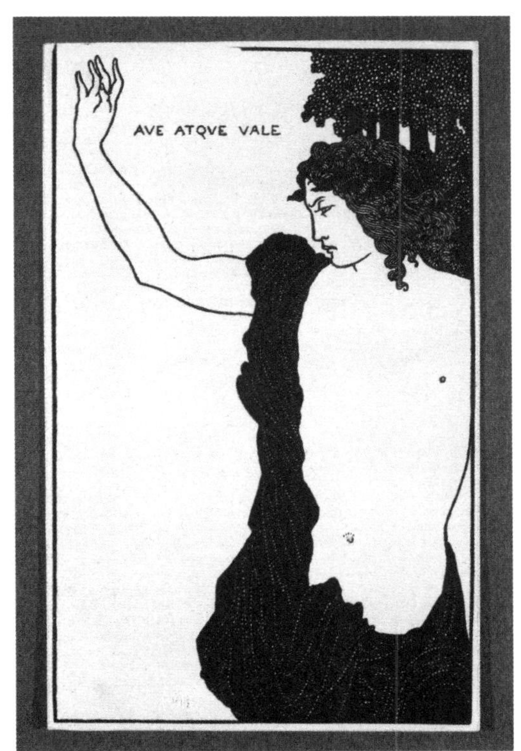

76. *Ave atque vale*, published in *The Savoy*, no. 7, 1896
Line block print
Victoria and Albert Museum, London
(V&A: E.433-1899)

Overleaf Vignette from *Bon-Mots of Samuel Foote and Theodore Hook*, edited by Walter Jerrold and published by J.M. Dent & Co., London, 1894, p. 113
Pen and ink on paper
Victoria and Albert Museum, London
(V&A: E.331-1972)

'Hail and farewell.' Published in *The Savoy* with Beardsley's translation of Catullus's elegy (Carmen 101) on the premature death of his brother, this image is also apt for its illustrator, who died on 16 March 1898, aged 25.

'I have worked to amuse myself, and if it has amused the public as well, so much the better for me'

1896

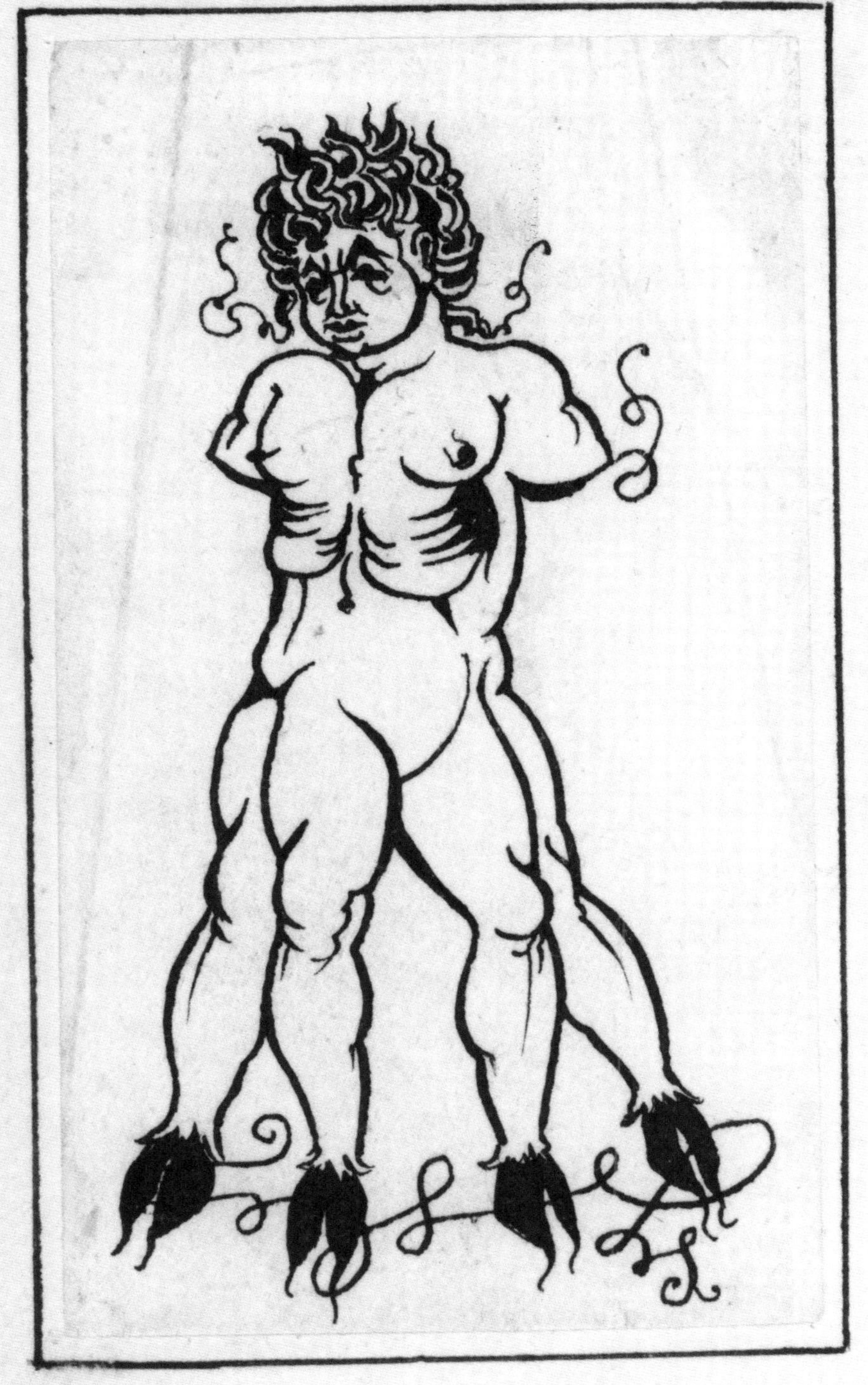

Notes

1 Sturgis 1998, p. 112

2 Simon Poe, review in *British Art Journal*, vol. 19, no. 3 (2018), p. 120

3 Aubrey Beardsley, quoted by Arthur Lawrence, *The Idler* (March 1897), quoted in Sturgis 1998, p. 309

4 Aubrey Beardsley to Frederick Evans, 20 August 1894, quoted in Anne Hammond, ed., *Frederick H. Evans: Selected Texts* (Oxford, 1992), p. 150. The photo was exhibited at the Linked Ring in 1894

5 Sturgis 1998, p. 2

6 Arthur Symons, *The Art of Aubrey Beardsley* (New York, 1918), preface

7 Maas et al. 1970, p. 27

8 Pearson 1946, p. 204

9 Symons 1918 (cited note 6)

10 Maas et al. 1970, p. 23

11 Ibid., p. 22

12 Ibid.

13 Ibid., p. 44

14 Ibid. Design published in *The Studio* (April 1893)

15 Maas et al. 1970, p. 44

16 Ibid., p. 55

17 Ibid., p. 45

18 Lago 1982, p. 174

19 Oscar Wilde to Aubrey Beardsley (March 1893), on a copy of *Salome* in the Sterling Library, Senate House, University of London

20 *The Times* (8 March 1894), p. 12

21 Publisher's prospectus for *The Yellow Book*

22 . As reported by Beerbohm to K.L. Mix (24 June 1930): Hart-Davis 1988, p. 176

23 Calloway 1998, p. 107

24 Hart-Davis 1962, p. 354

25 *Punch* (3 February 1895)

26 *To-Day* (12 May 1894), pp. 28–9

27 Ross 1909, pp. 38–9

28 Lago 1982, p. 174

29 Yeats 1955, p. 323

30 Maas et al. 1970, p. 79. No such drawing is known

31 Yeats 1955, pp. 329–30

32 Ibid., p. 321

33 Reported by Charles Ricketts, and quoted in Philippe Jullian, *Dreamers of Decadence: Symbolist Painters of the 1890s* (London, 1971), p. 257

34 Lago 1982, p. 187

35 Arthur Symons, *Aubrey Beardsley*, 1898, p. 13

36 Pennell 1911, pp. 310–11

37 Quoted in Calloway 1998, p. 206

38 Sturgis 1998, p. 290

39 Stephen Calloway, quoted by Martin Fuller, 'A dandy who makes dated seem cutting-edge', *New York Times* (11 October 1998), p. 2002037

40 The English version published by Smithers was ascribed to the otherwise unknown 'Samuel Smith', which may have been an alias

41 Sturgis 1998, p. 197

42 MS note dated 7 January 1898, Gallatin Beardsley Collection, Manuscript Division, Princeton University Library

43 Ross 1909, p. 17

44 Princeton University Library (AM 21318)

45 A.W. King, formerly of Brighton College

46 Maas et al. 1970, p. 22

47 D.S. MacColl, *The Spectator* (22 April 1893), pp. 523–4

48 *The Tablet*, supplement (11 March 1893), p. 5

49 Maas et al. 1970, p. 43

50 Theodore Wratislaw, 'Some drawings of Aubrey Beardsley', *The Artist and Journal of Home Culture* (September 1893), pp. 259–60

51 Lorraine Janzen Kooistra, 'Beardsley's reading of Malory's "Morte Darthur": images of a Decadent world', *Mosaic*, vol. 23, no. 1 (winter 1990), pp. 55–72

52 Maas et al. 1970, p. 43

53 Wratislaw (cited note 49), p. 260

54 Beardsley to T.D. Keighley (May 1893); Maas et al. 1970, p. 48

55 Thomas Malory, *Le Morte Darthur*, Book 19, Chapter 1

56 Ibid.

57 Lago 1982, p. 174

58 Ibid, p. 187

59 John Lewis May, *John Lane and the Nineties* (London, 1936), p. 74

60 P.G. Hamerton, quoted in *Magazine of Art*, no. 20 (1896)

61 Ibid.

62 Max Beerbohm, *Letters to Reggie Turner* (London, 1964), p. 87

63 Kenneth Clark, ed., *The Best of Aubrey Beardsley* (London, 1978), p. 36

64 Beardsley, *Caprice*, https://www.tate.org.uk/art/artworks/beardsley-caprice-verso-masked-woman-with-a-white-mouse-n03815 (accessed 26 April 2019)

65 Arthur Symons, 'Dieppe 1895', *The Savoy*, no. 1 (January 1896)

66 Allegedly based on the dancer Cleo de Merode

67 Reade 1967, p. 18

68 Maas et al. 1970, p. 150

69 Pennell 1911, pp. 310–11

70 Maas et al. 1970, p. 413 (from Mentone)

71 Ibid.

Picture Credits

Unless otherwise noted, all works reproduced in this book are in the Victoria and Albert Museum's collection, including those purchased with Art Fund Support: 42, 47, 50, 51, 54, 60, 61, 95, 107, 108, 109, 113, 114, 115, 117, 118, 126–7, 129, 130, 131, 132 and 139.

The other works are reproduced by kind permission of: © The Trustees of the British Museum: 10, 38, 44; © National Portrait Gallery: 11; © President and Fellows of Harvard College: 63; © Royal Academy of Arts, London: 120, 121, 124, 125; © Tate, London 2019: 40, 92, 93; The Picture Art Collection/Alamy Stock Photo: 69

Bon-Mots quotes

p.94 Letter from Aubrey Beardsley to the editor of *St Paul's Magazine*, 28 June 1895

p.106 Interview with Aubrey Beardsley in *To-Day*, 1894

p.16 Letter from Aubrey Beardsley to Brandon Thomas, May 1895

p.138 Interview with Aubrey Beardsley in *The Idler*, 1896

Selected Bibliography

Max Beerbohm, *A Variety of Things* (New York, 1928)

Brigid Brophy, *Black and White: A Portrait of Aubrey Beardsley* (London, 1969)

Brigid Brophy, *Beardsley and His World* (London, 1996)

Stephen Calloway, *Aubrey Beardsley* (V&A Publications, London, 1998)

Stephen Calloway and Susan Owens, *Aubrey Beardsley* (Tate Britain, London, 2020)

Dennis Denisoff and Lorraine Kooistra, eds, *The Yellow Nineties Online*, http://www.1890s.ca/Default.aspx (accessed 26 April 2019)

Jane Desmarais, *Monsters Under Glass: A Cultural History of Hothouse Flowers from 1850* (London, 2019)

Bram Djikstra, *Idols of Perversity* (Oxford, 1986)

Richard Ellmann, *Oscar Wilde* (London and New York, 1987)

Rupert Hart-Davis, ed., *The Letters of Oscar Wilde* (London, 1962)

Rupert Hart-Davis, ed., *More Letters of Oscar Wilde* (London, 1985)

Rupert Hart-Davis, ed., *The Letters of Max Beerbohm* (London, 1988)

Simon Heffer, *The Age of Decadence: Britain 1880–1914* (London, 2017)

Joris-Karl Huysmans, *Against Nature (Au Rebours)* (1884)

Holbrook Jackson, *The Eighteen Nineties* (London, 1913)

Mary Lago, ed., *Burne-Jones Talking* (London, 1982)

Mark S. Lasner, *Selective Checklist of Published Work by Aubrey Beardsley* (Boston, 1995)

Henry Maas, J.L. Duncan and W.G. Good, eds, *The Letters of Aubrey Beardsley* (London, 1970)

Catherine Maxwell, *Scents and Sensibility: Perfume in Victorian Literary Culture* (Oxford, 2012)

Hesketh Pearson, *Oscar Wilde, His Life and Wit* (London and New York, 1946)

Elizabeth R. and Joseph Pennell, *The Life of James McNeill Whistler* (London, 1911)

Brian Reade, *Aubrey Beardsley* (Victoria and Albert Museum, London, 1967)

Robert Ross, *Aubrey Beardsley* (London, 1909)

Chris Snodgrass, *Aubrey Beardsley: Dandy of the Grotesque* (Oxford, 1995)

Matthew Sturgis, *Aubrey Beardsley: A Biography* (London, 1998)

Matthew Sturgis, *Oscar: A Life* (London, 2018)

Arthur Symons, *Aubrey Beardsley*, (London, 1898)

Arthur Symons, *Aubrey Beardsley*, revised edition (London, 1905)

Arthur Symons, *The Art of Aubrey Beardsley* (New York, 1918)

Arthur Symons, 'Studies in strange sins (after the designs of Aubrey Beardsley)', in *Love's Cruelty* (London, 1923)

Stanley Weintraub, *Beardsley: A Biography* (London, 1967)

Simon Wilson and Linda G. Zatlin, *Aubrey Beardsley: A Centenary Tribute* (Tokyo, 1998)

W.B. Yeats, *Autobiographies* (London, 1955)

Linda G. Zatlin, *Aubrey Beardsley and Victorian Sexual Politics* (Oxford, 1990)

Linda G. Zatlin, *Aubrey Beardsley: A Catalogue Raisonné*, 2 vols (London and New York, 2016)

Acknowledgments

The author wishes to thank all those whose writings and views have informed and been consulted during the preparation of this title, including those listed in the Selected Bibliography, and especially Stephen Calloway, Colin Cruise and Susan Owens.

Thanks also to those involved in the editing, design and production of this publication: Hannah Newell, Ana Debenedetti and Zorian Clayton at the Victoria and Albert Museum, and Isabel Roldán and Julian Honer at Thames & Hudson.

Author's Biography

Jan Marsh is a biographer and curator specializing in Victorian art and culture. She has written biographies of Christina and Dante Gabriel Rossetti, Jane and May Morris and Elizabeth Siddal. Exhibition credits include *Pre-Raphaelite Women Artists* (Manchester City Art Gallery, 1995–6), *Black Victorians* (Manchester City Art Gallery, 2005 and Birmingham City Museum and Art Gallery, 2006), *Poetry in Beauty: The Pre-Raphaelite Art of Marie Spartali Stillman* (Delaware Art Museum, 2015–16) and *Pre-Raphaelite Sisters: Models, Artists, Muses* (National Portrait Gallery, London, 2019). She has also contributed extensively to the online National Portrait Gallery catalogue of later Victorian Portraits.

Front cover image: The Peacock Skirt, 1907 (p. 74)
Back cover image: The Climax, 1907 (p. 83)
Opposite title page: *A Foot-Note (Self-Portrait)*, published in *The Savoy*, no. 2, April 1896
Opposite contents page: Design for a chapter heading for *Le Morte Darthur*, 1893–4

First published in 2020 in hardcover in the United States of America by Thames & Hudson Inc., 500 Fifth Avenue, New York, New York 10110

www.thamesandhudsonusa.com

Library of Congress Control Number 2019940731

ISBN 978-0-500-480595

Printed and bound in China by C&C Offset Printing Co. Ltd

V&A Publishing

Supporting the world's leading museum of art and design, the Victoria and Albert Museum, London